The Art of the Possible:
Create an Organization with No Limitations

Daniel M. Jacobs, CPCM, CMC

Federal
Market
Publishing

Published by Federal Market Publishing, a company of The
Federal Market Group

ISBN: 1449961355
ISBN-13: 9781449961350

Library of Congress Control Number: 2010921052

TOPIC:

An integrated leadership and management guide to success. Specific steps that can be taken to improve performance in any organization. Focus is on the positive and the possible using seven practical and proven best practices. Combines best practices in leadership techniques and management processes.

STYLE/APPROACH:

Seven Best Practices, a chapter for each, detailed with real-world examples and success stories. Each chapter contains guidelines and checklists, with a self-assessment tool for each best practice. The objective is to move the reader to action.

TARGET AUDIENCE:

Today's developing young leader. Mid-level to Sr. Management personnel in large and small businesses, professional and civic organizations, government agencies, non-profits, and entrepreneurs – men and women – who aspire to leadership positions.

ADVANCE PRAISE:

"Dan Jacobs' profound understanding of leadership and management - how the two differ and how each can best be applied in conjunction with the other - has produced literally billions of dollars in success for his clients. The Art of the Possible charts that path to success for all who are willing to work hard enough to follow it." **-- Jed Babbin, former Deputy Undersecretary of Defense and Editor, Human Events.**

"This is not just another business book. This is a must read for anyone interested in building and improving an organization or managing a project to success. Dan Jacobs understands people and what motivates them to succeed. He also understands better than anyone I know how to bring people and processes together." **-- Michael Dallas, Chief Operating Officer, Thomas Jefferson National Accelerator Facility**

"What I like most about The Art of the Possible: Create an Organization with No Limitations is that it is so very practical. Seven steps to help you be more successful—not buzzwords or "flavors-of-the-month" but seven proven best practices, each fully explained with examples, guidelines, and checklists and personal action plan scorecards. It's easy to read, clearly written, well illustrated, and concise. And, it's the kind of book that you return to again and again, the kind of book that you really use to solve real problems and achieve real and lasting success. With The Art of the Possible, Dan has put into words what he has taught to thousands—with amazing results." **-- Randal Wotring, President, EG&G**

"Dan Jacobs' The Art of the Possible: Create an Organization with No Limitations does more than just combine proven best practices in leadership techniques and management processes. He quickly charts a relentless course for suc-

cess using a step-by-step, straight-forward, no-nonsense approach for the creation of an organization with no limits. He offers clear, powerful guidelines, checklists and self-assessment tools to help any leader succeed - especially in high stakes environments where just being good is not good enough!" -- **Frank J. Anderson, Jr., President, Defense Acquisition University**

"Dan's book provides a cogent set of building blocks for becoming an effective leader. If you master his Art of the Possible, your desired outcome for any action or activity you pursue will not only be possible, but probable." -- **Brent Armstrong, EVP, Performance Results Corporation**

"The Art of the Possible: Create an Organization with No Limitations provides the reader a proven primer for success. This isn't your ordinary business tome; it is a profound statement of what is necessary to build and sustain a world class organization. Read it, follow it – it works" -- **Edward V. Garlich, Jr., Founder/Managing Director, Washington Research Group**

Dan Jacobs' book is a treasure trove of insights, concepts and ideas that every aspiring manager should come to understand, appreciate and practice. The book is laced with lessons and experiences articulated by a remarkable array of corporate, government, sport leaders and even philosophers. The only possible weakness of this terrific text is that the reader cannot enjoy seeing and hearing Dan's persuasive, personable and powerful presentation of the fundamental and essential insights and suggestions presented in this book. It is a "must read."-- **Timothy J. Waters, Esq., Partner, McDermott Will & Emery**

The Art of the Possible:
Create an Organization with No Limitations

1. GET FOCUSED
2. SURROUND YOURSELF WITH TALENT
3. THINK STRATEGICALLY
4. FORGE A HIGH-PERFORMANCE TEAM
5. MANAGE THE FUNDAMENTALS
6. MAINTAIN DISCIPLINE
7. COMMUNICATE

CONTENTS

About the Author   i
Acknowledgements   iii
Foreword   v
Introduction   vii

Art of the Possible Best Practice #1   **3**
GET FOCUSED!

Introduction   5
Define and Passionately Pursue Your Vision –
     Your Preferred Future   5
Define and Live Your Values   6
Define Your Business Mission   8
Define Your Value Proposition   9
     (Unique Selling Proposition)
Clearly Define Your Goals/Objectives – Focus   10
Communicate – Up, Down & Out   11
Summary   14
FOCUS Application Model   15
Self-Assessment Checklist   16

Art of the Possible Best Practice #2   **21**
SURROUND YOURSELF WITH TALENT

Introduction   23
Value Principle & Energy Over Experience   24
Embrace Diversity in the Workplace   26
Focus on Results – Demand Excellence   26
Establish Centers of Excellence – Champion
     Teamwork   27
Identify and Build Leaders   29
Engage Every Mind – Make Them Stakeholders   29
Provide for Personal Growth   30
Summary   33
Self-Assessment Check   34

Art of the Possible Best Practice #3   **39**
THINK STRATEGICALLY

Introduction   41
Institutionalize and Champion Strategic Thinking
      & Planning   42
Strategic Planning – The Process   43
Where are we now? A Checklist.   46
Where do we want (need) to be? A Checklist.   47
How do we get there? A Checklist.   48
Who will take us there? A Checklist.   49
How are we doing? A Checklist.   50
Strategic Plan Outline   52
Manage the Plan – A Strategic Model   53
Summary   53
Self-Assessment Checklist   55

Art of the Possible Best Practice #4   **61**
FORGE A HIGH PERFORMANCE TEAM

Introduction   63
What to require from every Team Member   64
What to require from every Team Leader   65
Exploiting the Potential – Recipe for Success   66
Stages in Team Development   67
The Most Effective Organization (MEO)   67
Fundamental Organizational Tasks –
      The Work Breakdown Structure (WBS)   69
Win-Win Performance Agreements   70
Summary   73
Self-Assessment Checklist   75

Art of the Possible Best Practice #5   **81**
MANAGE THE FUNDAMENTALS

Introduction   83
Identify Key Processes/Systems   84
Baseline Fundamental Processes and Conduct
     Continuous Process Improvement   85
Provide Effective and Practical Performance
     Support Tools   88
Utilize Integrated Teams for Process Development   90
Summary   93
Self-Assessment Checklist   94

Art of the Possible Best Practice #6   **99**
MAINTAIN DISCIPLINE

Introduction   101
Deliver Quality Every Day – Culture of Discipline   102
The Business Case for Project Management   104
Role of the Project Manager   107
Six Step Process for a Community of Practice   108
Summary   110
Self-Assessment Checklist   112

Art of the Possible Best Practice #7   **117**
COMMUNICATE!

Introduction   119
Communications Planning   121
Information Distribution   122
Performance Distribution   123
Manage Stakeholders   124
Summary   126
Self-Assessment Checklist   127

CONCLUSION   129
BIBLIOGRAPHY   131
INDEX   133

ABOUT THE AUTHOR:

Daniel M. Jacobs, CPCM, CMC

Recognized as one of the nation's leading authorities on public contracting, **Daniel M. Jacobs** is Chairman/CEO of *The Federal Market Group (FMG)* that includes *Government Business Solutions (GBS), Federal Market Publishing (FMP), and The Federal Market Institute (FMI)*, Washington, D. C. based organizations providing professional training, research, publishing and consulting services to government and industry in public contracts management. FMG also includes *The EuroMarket Group* based in Brussels, Belgium and *FMG Middle East* in Tel Aviv.

He is a Fellow, past National President (1987-88), recipient of The Charles A. Dana Distinguished Service Award, the Honorary Life Member Award and a member of the Executive Advisory Council of the National Contract Management Association (NCMA). He is Chairman Emeritus, Board of Trustees, of the non-profit foundation, Contract Management Institute (CMI) and Chairman, Board of Advisors of Excel Institute. He is a member of the Project Management Institute (PMI), a member of the Institute of Management Consultants (IMC), a member of the Professional Services Council (PSC) and he is a Life Member of The American Legion. Through examination, he earned the designation of *Certified Professional Contracts Manager (CPCM) and Certified Management Consultant (CMC)*. He served three years active duty with the U. S. Army and attained the rank of Captain.

He is principal author of *Building a Contract: Solicitations/ Bids and Proposals - A Team Effort?*, NCMA, 1990. He is the author of, *Federal Government Contracting: The System/The Process*, FMP, 1989, *The Integrated Project/Team (IPT)*, FMP, 2000, and *The Desktop Reference Guide for Contract Management, FMP, 2001*.

i

ACKNOWLEDGEMENTS

This book has been a long-time coming. The title was given to me by a good friend, *John Fairfield.* John is a highly decorated retired three-star Air Force General and a leader of legendary proportions. After retirement, he worked as a Vice President for DynCorp leading strategic planning.

We were working together on a project he conceived to address the challenge the Department of Defense (DOD) is facing regarding the soaring costs of maintaining the infrastructure of the aging military bases. His charge to me was to think through how we could make it possible. As a team, we co-authored the "DOD City-Base" concept where the federal government privatizes the base and the local community buys it, improves the infrastructure and leases it back to DOD – it works. He paid me a wonderful complement by saying that I practice the *Art of the Possible.* Thank you John.

I have the privilege of living a fulfilling life that is graced by work for which I have a passion and a number of people who influence that state of fulfillment. In the past and currently, I have been blessed with a loving family, good friends, insightful mentors, sharing acquaintances and professional colleagues.

Foremost in my life is my business and life partner, *Janet,* who for the past 48 years has provided only unselfish love, unqualified support and uncanny insight into people and processes. She was adamant that I complete this book and was my principal critic. She also helped me with the most important results of my life; my children, *Deana, Mercedes, Daniel and Adam.* They in turn have provided us with wonderful additions to our family with their partners: *Paris, Don and Alex.* Combined they have produced our seven grandchildren: *Joshua, Shane, Megan, Austin, Madison, Lillyan and Daniel III.* This book is dedicated to them, may they each practice the *Art of the Possible.*

A number of friends with considerable credentials reviewed this book and offered constructive comments and encouragement: *Frank Anderson, Brent Armstrong, Vick Avetissian, Jed Babbin, Fred Bowen, Mike Czarny, Mike Dallas, Gerry Decker, Gene Desaulniers, John Fairfield, Ed Garlich, Greg Garrett, Randy Kase, Idy Marcus, Don McPhee, Ben Medley, Steve Perry, Tom Reid, Jim Rider, Bonnie Ross, George Starke, Lenn Vincent, Tim Waters, Randy Wotring, Tom Wrenn and Phil Yenrick.* To each, my profound thanks.

Dan Jacobs

FOREWORD

By John S. Fairfield, Lt. Gen. USAF (Ret.)

I cherished the privilege of serving our Country as a member of the United States Air Force for thirty-five years. It's hard to explain why I had this passion for the Air Force to those who did not have the same opportunity. I often try to use a sports analogy and reference the great years of the Boston Celtics and their legendary coach Arnold "Red" Auerbach. Coach Auerbach made individual stars play as a team. In one eulogy, he was described as "a master tactician, amateur psychologists, and a shrewd judge of talent, whose intelligence and strong acerbic personality kept him in complete control of his team and usually two or three steps ahead of the opposition."

Upon reaching military retirement, I was led to a magnificent employee-owned company, DynCorp, who had as one of their business consultants, Dan Jacobs. Dan was teaching a course in program management which I decided to monitor. It only took me a few minutes to exclaim to myself that Dan Jacobs was using Red Auerbach's play book. He wasn't just preaching the fundamentals of program management; he was teaching this class how to be a team. I knew immediately that a company that recognized the talents of a master teacher like Dan Jacobs was a company that I could unequivocally support.

Like everything else he touches, Dan Jacobs helped DynCorp achieve a remarkable record of employee satisfaction and enviable business growth. The readers of this book will get the benefit of his expertise and should come away with a renewed sense of self focus if they follow these seven principles of leadership. Dan makes these seven "best practices" plain because he is a life- long practitioner of the art of leadership. Those of us who have been in the military and have had the experience of being part of the "profession of arms" know that leadership is expected, found and nurtured at all ranks.

In this brilliantly simple book, Dan integrates these seven best practices into a cohesive pattern that will support the beginning employee and refine the talents of the seasoned executive if carefully followed.

I had the privilege of working and traveling with Dan on important business opportunities during which we challenged our audiences with thinking out of the box to get to their objectives. During these engagements, I saw Dan's leadership in action. As a leader, Dan does three things extremely well, he TRUSTS, he LISTENS, he THANKS. As you read this book, you'll find these and other qualities threaded into a very cohesive web of excellence.

Thank you, Dan, for writing this down and sharing what you know with others. This book puts a little science into the art of the possible!

Author's Note:
Lt. General John J. Fairfield, a legendary leader, is rated as a pilot, navigator and bombardier. Included in his many decorations and awards is the "Order of the Sword" from Air Force Noncommissioned Officers which recognizes individuals who have made significant contributions to the enlisted corps. Other recipients include Bob Hope, Gen. Curtis LeMay and Casper Weinberger. John practices The Art of the Possible.

INTRODUCTION

> *"Gentlemen, we are going to relentlessly chase perfection, knowing full well we will not catch it, because nothing is perfect. But we are going to relentlessly chase it, because in the process we will catch excellence. I am not remotely interested in just being good."*
>
> *Hall of Fame Football Coach Vince Lombardi, Opening Remarks to his team as the new head coach of the Green Bay Packers (Five NFL Championships, Two Super Bowls)*

Most of us have worked in successful as well as unsuccessful organizations. Why does one succeed, the other fail?

There is an old saying, *"Lead, follow or get the hell out of the way"* that literally provides us the answer. In today's global and highly competitive marketplace, the successful organization must follow that old saw. **This book is about creating an organization where things get done, where anything is possible.** This book is about excellence and success!

To succeed, you are compelled to have an organization that is well led and peopled by principled and competent individuals that foster teamwork. To do otherwise, you place limitations on your organization and subsequently fail or do not realize your full potential.

This book represents an integrated leadership and management process that provides the reader with a proven and practical approach to success. It focuses on the positive – on what works. I call it practicing *the art of the possible; creating an organization with no limitations.*

The Art of the Possible is applicable to start-ups as well as established organizations challenged with change. It integrates seven key best practices in leadership and management into a step-by-step approach. It merges the ideal with the pragmatic. It offers guidelines, checklists and self-assessment tools to facilitate application of those best practices.

Best practices are defined as those processes, approaches and practices that have been successfully applied in a particular area of business or activity. A best practice is a proven approach to performance that, when applied in a consistent manner in similar activities, should produce successful results.

In an organization with no limitations, anything is possible; that is why we call it *the art of the possible.* It represents an organizational mindset and culture with an attitude where anything can be done, where anything is possible. Embrace and apply *the art of the possible*; it will work in any type of business or at any level in an organization.

For the past 30 years, I've had the privilege of working with a number of successful businesses, government agencies, professional and charitable non-profits and civic organizations. Conversely, I've observed or worked with many more that were dysfunctional and subsequently unsuccessful. Many of those that were once the best lost the magic, many of those that were the worst became better. Why does one succeed, the other fail?

The answer comes from a number of sources I have researched, interviewed or worked with during those 30 years. It always boils down to one irrefutable factor, *the leader.*

Certainly nothing is new or earth shattering in that discovery. Many successful leaders inspire us. Each has his or her own style and approach to leading. However, when examined closely, there are common practices and certain consistencies that appear quite regularly in the actions and approaches of leaders in successful organizations (best practices).

Of course the leader isn't the only factor contributing to success, but the successful leader creates an environment where all of the other factors have an opportunity to surface, be nurtured, and applied. These seven best practices create that environment; that culture.

What separates this book from other tomes on leadership is the step-by-step integrated approach that facilitates the creation of an organization with no limitations.

A brief look at several of the successful leaders referenced in this book who practice *the art of the possible* will give you some insight into what is in store for you when you read the rest of this practical guide to success in any organization.

They include: the late *David Packard*, co-founder and Chairman of Hewlett-Packard Corporation; Colonel *Steve Perry*, U.S. Army; *Dan Bannister*, former Chairman of DynCorp; and, *Jack Welch*, former Chairman and CEO of General Electric.

Also included are: *Elizabeth Hanford Dole*, former President of the American Red Cross; *Charles Schwab*, Chairman and CEO of Charles Schwab & Co., Inc.; and, *Beverly Milkman*, former Executive Director of the President's Committee on Purchasing from the Blind and Severely Disabled.

David Packard co-founded and grew Hewlett Packard into Silicon Valley's most admired organization and when called to chair a presidential advisory committee, he irrevocably changed the way the federal government conducts business.

Steve Perry, a young Army career officer, was given command of a dysfunctional organization with a critical national mission and resolutely turned it into a high-performance team.

Dan Bannister, faced with losing his company to corporate raiders, seized the day and led an employee buyout that turned DynCorp into a world leader in information and technical services.

Jack Welch, recognized as perhaps the greatest CEO of the last century, took over a very profitable but hidebound General Electric and turned it into one of the world's most valuable enterprises with a $300 billion-plus market capitalization.

Elizabeth Dole assumed leadership of The American Red Cross after distinguished service as Secretary of Labor and Transportation. Instead of coasting through her tenure as president of the venerable non-profit, she chose to awaken the slumbering bureaucracy of 30,000 full-time employees and hundreds of thousands of volunteers. In the process, she saved the organization more than $140 million in operating costs in less than two years.

Charles Schwab sold his company in 1984 to Bank of America. Unhappy with what he saw them doing with his company – they literally changed the character and culture – he bought the company back. Today, Charles Schwab & Co. is the largest discount brokerage firm ($300 billion) in the nation.

Beverly Milkman ran one of the U.S. Government's smallest executive agencies (19 full-time personnel), but one with a significant and challenging mission, The President's Committee for Purchasing from the Blind and Severely Disabled.

She personifies the new breed of government leaders and has led award-winning changes at the Committee.

A brief example of success stories, but common to all is that mindset, that attitude – it can be done, anything is possible. They created organizations with no limitations; they practice the *art of the possible.*

I've taken the best practices used by those and other leaders and integrated them into a comprehensive guide to facilitate creation of your own organizational culture with no limitations – an organization that practices the art of the possible.

It's my sincere hope that this book will move you to action. In any event, lead, follow or get out of the way!

Daniel M. Jacobs
Washington, D.C.

The Art of the Possible:
Create an Organization with No Limitations

1. GET FOCUSED
2. SURROUND YOURSELF WITH TALENT
3. THINK STRATEGICALLY
4. FORGE A HIGH-PERFORMANCE TEAM
5. MANAGE THE FUNDAMENTALS
6. MAINTAIN DISCIPLINE
7. COMMUNICATE

Art of the Possible Best Practice #1
GET FOCUSED!

"You know that the beginning is the most important part of any work, especially in the case of a young and tender thing; for that is the time at which the character is being formed and the desired impression is more readily taken. . . ."

– Plato's Republic

Introduction   5
Define and Passionately Pursue Your Vision –
    Your Preferred Future   5
Define and Live Your Values   6
Define Your Business Mission   8
Define Your Value Proposition
    (Unique Selling Proposition)   9
Clearly Define Your Goals/Objectives – Focus   10
Communicate – Up, Down & Out   11
Summary   14
FOCUS Application Model   15
Self-Assessment Checklist   16

INTRODUCTION

This first best practice is the most critical in successful organizations. The root cause of any successful endeavor can be traced to a leader that is focused. The first step in creating an organization with no limitations is to have a clear understanding of what you want to accomplish and then zealously focus on that quest.

Fundamental to creating your organizational culture with no limitations is to articulate your vision of what you want the organization to be. Define your organization's preferred future.

Concurrent with that effort, it is essential to define the core principles or values by which you and your personnel will conduct themselves, what you want your organization to accomplish (mission), what is unique about your product and services (value proposition) and the specific goals and objectives you will work together to attain.

You are establishing a standard by which you and your organization will measure success. Once these have been clearly articulated, continually communicate them to your people and then passionately pursue them. They are the very soul of your organization.

You are focused. It is the beginning.

VISION

Much has been written about what a vision is or isn't, but one thing is certain, the old Sioux proverb is correct, *"if you don't know where you are going, any path will take you there."*

Your vision is a clear picture of where and what you want your organization to be in the future (1-5 years). It provides all the players a clear target. You begin the teambuilding process by establishing a preferred future. From the moment you establish your vision, your resources are focused within the framework of that vision.

Your vision is your organization's challenge to succeed. It is the foundation of your organization. Your message to your people is clear – "*I know where we are going and I want you to help me get there!*"

If you cannot articulate your vision, seek advice. Internally, have your key personnel help you by brainstorming and determining what the organization's preferred future must be. Externally, if you are a start-up, try to find a mentor or someone who can advise you. It is essential that your vision is clearly stated and everyone in the organization knows where you and they are going. Google vision or mission statement on the internet for an abundance of sample vision and mission statements.

Visions do not become reality by caveat. Your organization must understand and believe in your vision. Simply placing placards and posters in strategic locations and occasional homage to the idea will not make it happen. You must establish clear goals and metrics that will facilitate attaining your vision. Hold yourself and your personnel accountable to your vision. Focus!

John (Jack) Welch, Jr., former CEO/Chairman of General Electric, defines it this way, "*Good business leaders create a vision, articulate the vision, passionately own the vision, and relentlessly drive it to completion.*"

VALUES
Your values, or core principles, are the fundamental, unchanging rules of conduct that will govern all of your own actions and those of your personnel. These must be articulated, communicated and enforced. You can't seek advice

on this. If you do not genuinely believe and practice them, they will not work.

Integrity – requires the highest standards of ethical and moral conduct. Stephen Covey defines it as *"a promise made is a promise kept."* No other single value will serve you better. Your word is your bond.

Respect for People – Everyone in the organization must treat one another with honesty, fairness and respect. In today's workplace, there are no subordinates – only team-mates. Be a community of people who support and care for one another. It's about treating people right. Every job is important, every person is important.

Management By Fact – minimize assumptions. Deal in facts not innuendo, assumptions and hearsay. Continually pursue facts and relevant information for decision-making. Move swiftly on issue resolution.

Empowerment – delegate responsibility and authority; create an environment where decision-making is at the lowest level possible; stimulate and encourage initiative in one another; continually review processes and policies to streamline operations. Ensure that everyone is involved. Every job is important, every person is important!

Passion/Enthusiasm – convey and sustain a genuine love for your work and life in general. Enjoy! It is contagious.

Teamwork/Partnership – share knowledge and resources across organizations; cooperate with one another and work together toward common goals; work as a team to solve problems and improve processes. Whenever possible, provide incentives and/or equity.

Quality – meet or exceed customer requirements; form close working partnerships with customers and suppliers; continually improve products and processes. Be obsessive about quality and customer focus!

Innovation – challenge the status quo and encourage prudent risk taking; value new ideas anticipate change; lead change; strive for speed and simplicity in carrying out work.

Fulfillment – take pride in work and celebrate accomplishments; strive for personal satisfaction to meet customer and organization needs, work together to enhance shareholder value through profitable growth.

You are building a solid foundation for your organization. Lead by example. Live your values!

MISSION
Clearly define the purpose of your organization. Define the arena of: products, services, customers, technologies, and geography in which you will compete to get results.

If you are managing a non-business or non-profit enterprise, substitute the above with a clear definition of the purpose of your organization, why your organization exits and the end results you must accomplish to be successful.

Your vision sets forth what you want your organization to be in the future, your mission establishes why you exist. Your vision focuses you on the future; your mission focuses you on the day-to-day operations.

A clearly articulated mission forces you to allocate your resources to get the best results. If your mission is too broad, then your resources could be too dispersed to be effective and therefore used unwisely with poor results. If your mission is too narrow, you could under utilize your resources and drive up costs. Think productivity!

A well-defined mission statement facilitates market research and identification of competitors and market forces impacting your organization.

Sample Mission Statement: *The Federal Market Group (FMG) provides a focal-point and resource for those conducting business utilizing public contracts in federal, state and international government organizations. FMG provides consulting services and professional training; conducts research and develops materials to assist those organizations – government and industry.*

By clearly defining the arena of products, services, customers, technologies and geography in which you will compete, you make better informed decisions about resources in areas such as personnel, skill mixes, funding, costs, profit margins, pricing, time, facilities, equipment, support systems and internal processes.

Your mission focuses your resources and drives your goals and objectives.

VALUE PROPOSITION

What is it about your products and services that set you apart from the competition? You must determine what your unique selling proposition is and clearly articulate that message in all of your promotional materials and advertising.

Why should your organization be chosen over your competitor? If you can't answer that question, how can you expect your customer to know the answer?

Example: *"With FMG, You Win!"* Then validate it with facts.

GOALS/OBJECTIVES

Goals and objectives in this context are interchangeable and can be defined as results necessary to achieve your organization's mission. Goals define success for the organization. They can be both quantitative and qualitative.

Once again an old saw is applicable, *"what gets measured gets done."* Goals establish specific metrics for your organization and allow all the players to understand how you define success.

Goals that are well-defined goal should be **SMART**:

<u>S</u>pecific – there is no room for ambiguity in articulating a goal. A goal must include specific metrics that are both quantitative and qualitative and are consistent with your organization's vision, values and mission.

<u>M</u>easurable – What gets measured get done! Establish milestones, monetary amounts, percentage points; a measurable goal.

<u>A</u>ttainable – a goal must be realistic and reflect a rational decision-making process that challenges the organization but is also attainable, or it will have a negative effect.

<u>R</u>elevant – you must validate a goal before establishing it. Insure that it is not ambiguous and there is buy-in by the entire organization.

<u>T</u>rackable – establish milestones and metrics for each goal and follow progress.

Goals can be categorized as:

<u>Strategic Goals</u> – The big picture. Specific results necessary to implement the organization's strategic plan to reach

its vision and to achieve the mission. The big picture, reflects your strategic, operational and project goals to meet your near-term (6-18 months) and long-term (18 months to 3-5 years) objectives.

Operational Goals – specific results necessary to meet operational day-to-day mission requirements in accordance with the strategic goals.

Team/Project Goals – specific results necessary to meet scope, quality, time, and cost and customer satisfaction set forth in a contract or task. Projects are defined as requirements with specific time frames for a beginning and end.

Individual Goals – specific results necessary for each individual to develop personally and to fully understand their role and responsibilities in the organization. These goals will, in turn, accomplish project, operational and strategic goals. Performance agreements and career development are essential elements.

Examples of SMART goals:
1.   Increase manufacturing productivity by 12% over the next 12 months and by 20% within three years. (Stra tegic Goal)
2.   Increase sales: $6M in Bookings, $3M in Revenue for FY 2XXX. (Operational Goal)
3.   New Operating System: Launch Feb.1, 2XXX, Com plete NLT Aug. 15, 2XXX (Team/Project Goal)
4.   Sit for Project Management Professional (PMP) Ex amination within the next 12 months. (Individual Goal)

COMMUNICATE! UP, DOWN and OUT.
When you articulate your vision, baseline your values, define your mission and establish your goals you are on a compass heading to success, however, if you do not clearly commu-

nicate them to your personnel, you will have accomplished nothing except a rather exhaustive academic exercise.

Everyone in the organization must embrace your vision, live the values, focus on the mission and work as a team to meet goals. Those who do not should not be tolerated in your organization.

To communicate your vision, values, and mission is an on-going effort. This requires a communications plan. **Best Practice # 7 – Communicate**, sets forth the steps necessary to develop and execute a Communications Plan. It need not be cumbersome and lengthy to be effective, but there must be an organization-wide effort to maintain focus. The commitment to vision, values, mission and goals should be a daily mantra at every level.

Certainly posters, placards, etc. facilitate the communication process, but the most effective communication tool is one-on-one. Every new team member should be briefed upon entry to the organization and required to discuss their understanding and commitment to the vision, values, mission and goals.

Periodic meetings to discuss personal goals should reinforce the message and those who choose not to focus should be held accountable. Individual performance agreements should reflect commitment to the vision, values, mission and goals. **Best Practice # 4 – Forge a High Performance Team**, addresses this critical function in more detail.

Michael Dell, Chairman/CEO Dell Computers is perhaps the finest example of a leader who follows this practice best. Focused from the beginning, Michael Dell founded Dell Computers in 1984.

While in high school, he discovered computers and by the time he was in college, he was selling them out of his dorm room. From that first sale to now, his focus has been on selling computers direct to customers who call Dell on the phone or order on the internet.

He also is focused on efficient manufacturing, quality products and quality personnel. He revolutionized computer sales. Every individual in his organization knows exactly what Dell's vision, values, mission and goals are. He is rated by many as one the best CEOs in America, Dell has grown his company to more than $18 billion annually and 24,000 employees. He practices the Art of the Possible!

Dan Bannister, former Chairman/CEO of DynCorp, a leading worldwide telecommunications and service provider, is another outstanding example of the application of this best practice.

Shortly after concluding an employee buyout, Bannister established a 5-year Strategic Plan for DynCorp in which he set forth goals to reduce debt incurred in the buyout, improve profitability, diversify corporate products, increase the customer base and create an employee ownership culture.

Previously, DynCorp, then a 40-year old company, enjoyed an excellent reputation in providing facilities and engineering support to the Department of Defense and a few other federal government agencies. Bannister, however, recognized that the market was changing and he must lead radical change in his company.

He and his management team developed an ambitious 5-year strategic plan. In the introduction to that plan, Bannister stated, "*Perhaps the greatest challenge of all will be to represent things not as we wish them to be but rather to dare dream of things that must come to past.*" He understood that DynCorp's 18,000 employee-owners must be focused.

At the end of five years DynCorp had reduced its debt by 60%, increased profitability to historic highs, transitioned the company to a high-tech information technology provider while expanding its customer base 10-fold in support services. He practices the Art of the Possible!

SUMMARY

Once you are focused, you'll find that you have begun a journey with clearly defined directions on how to get there. You are now ready for the next best practice – **SURROUND YOURSELF WITH TALENT! Establish Centers of Excellence.**

Review the FOCUS Application model and complete the **Art of the Possible Best Practice #1 GET FOCUSED** Self Assessment Checklist. Determine how you will reach "5's" for every requirement.

You are focused. It is the beginning.

Focus Application Model
It all begins with you clearly knowing what you want your organization to be!

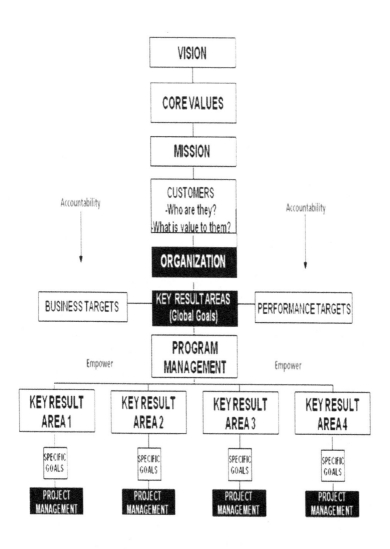

Art of the Possible Best Practice #1
GET FOCUSED!

CHECKLIST & PERSONAL ACTION PLAN SCORECARD

Focus Areas	Score	What Do You Need?	How Will You Do It?	When?
Vision: 1. Clear statement of your preferred future 2. Included Key Personnel in development 3. Communication Plan includes focus on Vision				
Values: 1. Integrity 2. Respect for People 3. Management by Fact 4. Empowerment 5. Passion/Energy 6. Quality 7. Partnership 8. Innovation 9. Fulfillment 10. Communication Plan includes focus on Values				
Mission: 1. Clear Mission Statement 2. Defined Products 3. Defined Services 4. Defined Technologies 5. Defined Geography 6. Communication Plan includes focus on Mission				

Art of the Possible Best Practice #1
GET FOCUSED!

CHECKLIST & PERSONAL ACTION
PLAN SCORECARD (Continued)

Focus Areas	Score	What Do You Need?	How Will You Do It?	When?
Goals: 1. Quantitative 2. Qualitative 3. Specific 4. Attainable 5. Validated 6. Easily Tracked 7. Strategic Goals 8. Operational Goals 9. Project Goals 10. Individual Goals 11. Communication Plan includes focus on Goals				
Communication Plan 1. Internal 2. External				
Scale: 0 – No Focus 1 – Thought about it 2 – Discussed it 3 – Partially Completed 4 – Articulated, Written, Validated 5 – Completed, Communicating & Practicing		**Your Action Plan to Achieve "5's" Across the Board**		

The Art of the Possible:
Create an Organization with No Limitations

1. GET FOCUSED
2. SURROUND YOURSELF WITH TALENT
3. THINK STRATEGICALLY
4. FORGE A HIGH-PERFORMANCE TEAM
5. MANAGE THE FUNDAMENTALS
6. MAINTAIN DISCIPLINE
7. COMMUNICATE

Art of the Possible Best Practice #2
SURROUND YOURSELF WITH TALENT

"If an organization is to maximize its efficiency and success, a number of requirements must be met. One is that the most capable people available should be selected for each assignment within the organization."

– David Packard, Hewlett Packard

Introduction	23
Value Principle & Energy Over Experience	24
Embrace Diversity in the Workplace	26
Focus on Results – Demand Excellence	26
Establish Centers of Excellence – Champion Teamwork	27
Identify and Build Leaders	29
Engage Every Mind – Make Them Stakeholders	29
Provide for Personal Growth	30
Summary	33
Self-Assessment Check	34

INTRODUCTION

Football Hall of Fame coach *Joe Gibbs*, winner of three Super Bowls as head coach of the Washington Redskins (with three different quarterbacks), began each year's training camp by saying to his players, *"The most important job I have is choosing the right people."*

To practice the *Art of the Possible* you must surround yourself with talent and then create centers of excellence where that talent can flourish. General Colin Powell calls it creating *"force multipliers"*. To attract talent, you must make some fundamental decisions early about what kind of organization you will lead and <u>who</u> will do what, when, where and how.

You are off to a good start by being *focused*. Your *vision, values, mission, value proposition and goals*, in fact, lay the *foundation* for the kind of organization you will lead. Your task now is to choose and nurture the best and brightest to help you get there.

Most successful organizations are those that build upon a talented, stable and dedicated workforce that share in the benefits of success. This best practice is really about values and treating people right.

Bill Hewlett and David Packard made that decision in 1947 at the outset of the formation of Hewlett Packard Corporation, Silicon Valley's most admired company. They *"did not want to be a 'hire and fire' – a company that would seek large, short-term contracts, employ a great many people for the duration of the contract, and at its completion let those people go."*

Hewlett and Packard wanted to create *"an environment that fostered individual motivation, initiative, and creativity, and that gave wide latitude of freedom in working toward common goals and objectives."* In addition, they determined benefits such as profit sharing would be provided to all eligible employees.

Like Gibbs and others, they correctly recognized that every person in the organization is important and every job is important.

Today's highly competitive marketplace demands quality products and services, but to be competitive, you must deliver them *faster, better, cheaper.* Hewlett's and Packard's approach was and is the standard to meet that challenge.

To attract talented people, you must create an organization that appeals to the skilled, knowledgeable, and principled individual. We all know that every person is motivated by different stimuli. However, most talented people are attracted to a form of participatory management that supports individual freedom and initiative while emphasizing commonness of purpose and teamwork along with recognition and rewards for successful performance.

In pursuing talent, you must convince the best and brightest that you value principle and energy over experience, you embrace diversity, you focus on results and you demand excellence. You build leaders and create centers of excellence. You champion teamwork, engage every mind in the organization, make everyone a stakeholder and provide for personal growth.

Create that kind of organization and you will attract, retain and grow talent. You are creating an organizational culture with no limitations. You are practicing the A*rt of the Possible.*

VALUE PRINCIPLES AND ENERGY OVER EXPERIENCE

You want to pick the best people who contribute most to meeting the vision, values, mission and goals of your organization. In doing so, you must value principle and energy over experience. Validate their core principles to ensure that they are compatible to yours and then validate their energy – their commitment and enthusiasm for life and their work.

An individual can have excellent technical, business, marketing, sales, financial or administrative skills with years of experience, but if they do not have core values that are compatible with yours, they will not fit. You can teach someone a skill, you can provide them with knowledge, but you most often cannot teach them fundamental principles such as integrity and respect for people.

You must also pick people who are excited about their work and who excite others – people with energy! They become *centers of excellence.*

I once observed *Eileen McCullough,* National Sales Manager for Dun & Bradstreet Business Education Services, at a trade show and was impressed by her team's consistent and highly professional conduct at their D&B booth. Eileen and her three teammates were all under 30. Representatives in other booths, of all ages, were enthusiastic, but appeared to lack a level of energy and commitment evident in the D&B crew.

I asked her why her young team was so attentive and professional. She replied that each of them had been selected based on character first and experience second. Each had demonstrated a strong work ethic, strong core values and was excited about their opportunity with D&B. Their exceptional performance validates her approach.

I inquired where she learned such sage advice at such a young age. She responded that she had a mentor in D&B who taught her. She values principles over experience. She is a center of excellence. She practices the *Art of the Possible.*

EMBRACE DIVERSITY IN THE WORKPLACE
Value and embrace diversity – you are not looking for your clones. Hire principled individuals with skills and knowledge that complement your vision, values, mission and goals. Recognize the wonderful ethnic and gender diversity of the nation and base selection on values, energy, talent and potential, only.

Lawrence Bossidy, former Chairman and CEO of AlliedSignal, put this in perspective when he said that you should *"fill your company with people who are bursting with energy and creativity; people with diverse talents, who nonetheless can work together in a team setting."*

Surround yourself with people who have strengths and insights that are different from yours!

FOCUS ON RESULTS – DEMAND EXCELLENCE
The key to productivity is to focus on results, not efforts. Define success and hold people accountable for results. Demand excellence – do not accept anything less.

Establish an organization that cares about the delivery of results. Ensure that everyone understands this philosophy and approach. Develop valid metrics and fair tools to measure results.

For *leaders*, establish performance agreements, metrics, and incentives, and then evaluate them using their *peers, customers, supervisor, and subordinates (this approach is often referred to as the 360° evaluation technique).*

For *teams*, establish team/project goals and hold each team member accountable for the end results and rewards. For *individuals*, establish performance agreements with specific metrics that are both qualitative and quantitative, include incentives.

Every person is important, every job is important. Each individual in your organization must clearly understand their roles and responsibilities and the standards by which they will be measured. When you hold someone accountable, they must understand the rules of the game. Do not operate on the basis of unknown expectations, define and baseline those expectations.

Accountability is a two-way street. If people are to be held accountable, they must be provided the resources and tools to accomplish the task.

ESTABLISH CENTERS OF EXCELLENCE – CHAMPION TEAMWORK

To create an environment that fosters individual motivation, initiative and creativity, establish *Centers of Excellence.* Centers of Excellence can be defined as organizations and teams of diverse members with common goals and objectives that are well led. Centers of Excellence can also be individuals. Identify those individuals and champion teamwork!

A Center of Excellence is an entrepreneurial organization or individual with focus, flexibility, and agility. They fully subscribe to the notion that the whole is greater than the sum of the parts and their efforts are an integral part of that whole.

Give individuals and teams wide latitude and freedom to accomplish their goals, reward them for success and hold them accountable for failure. They should have a strong sense of the vision, values, mission and goals of the larger organization and should establish their own vision, mission, and goals within that context for their own operations or projects.

Assign competent leaders to Centers of Excellence. You may call them business units, departments, divisions, programs, projects or teams, but the common element is their particular focus within the context of the organization's strategic goals.

In 1986, *David Packard*, co-founder of Hewlett Packard and Deputy Secretary of Defense under President Ford (Donald Rumsfeld was Secretary of Defense), was selected by President Reagan to chair the President's Blue Ribbon Commission on Defense Management. His charter was to find a better way to manage the huge Department of Defense (DOD).

His was probably the 40th such commission established over the years by various administrations. Most had little effect upon the operations of DOD; Packard, however, made a difference.

In his final report, which became known as the *"Packard Commission Report"*, he discussed the development of "centers of management excellence" in acquisition (procurement): *"The quest for excellence. . .will be successful only if a new management philosophy can replace the old. Instead of concentrating on the things that are being done wrong and trying to fix them with more laws, more regulations, and more inspectors. . .concentrate on those things that are done right and use them as models."*

In reviewing successful programs in DOD, Packard found four common attributes in each:
(1)   They were well led;
(2)   They were well planned:
(3)   They were performed by competent people; and
(4)   They performed as a Team.

Packard forever changed the government paradigm; he introduced them to Best Practices. As a result of the Packard Commission Report, subsequent Federal statutes and regulations mandate leadership training, planning, performance accountability, competency-based promotions, continuing training and education requirements and teamwork. Common sense: leadership, planning and competent people working as a team. *He practiced the Art of the Possible.*

IDENTIFY AND BUILD LEADERS

Leaders are at a premium. You must identify and build your own from within as much as possible. Establish formal career development, training, and mentoring programs to facilitate this important function.

Centers of Excellence are prime on-the-job training ground for future leaders. By assuming responsibility for their actions in teams, on projects and performing specific tasks, they are exposed to best practices. Allow them room to fail as well as to succeed.

Not everyone has leadership potential. Identify those that have potential early and provide them with counseling and guidance. For those without leadership potential, determine their strengths and facilitate growth in specialties that will meet their personal as well as your organizational goals.

PriceWaterhouseCoopers (PwC), one of nation's leading accounting and consulting firms, with annual revenues in excess of $25 billion and more than 146,000 personnel, recruits and trains more than 2800 Interns annually. They are consistently rated as the number one choice by college students because of their commitment to leadership development. *They practice the Art of the Possible.*

ENGAGE EVERY MIND – MAKE THEM STAKEHOLDERS

Jack Welch, states it very plainly "*use the brain of every worker.*" The men and women working on the line or providing services directly to the customer are closest to the work. They are where the creativity and innovation lay. Use that resource.

Often referred to as *empowerment*, it is involvement at every level. It simply ensures that your people are, in fact, a part of the decision-making process. It does not take away from the responsibilities of the leader. Someone still must make the final decision on what recommendations to use. Harnessing that incredible resource, however, is a priority.

One of the greatest motivators for people is to be part of the decision-making process. That makes them a stakeholder in the outcome. In most cases, they will be much more productive if they know that their ideas and opinions are valued.

Another effective approach to enhance productivity is to make them stakeholders through profit sharing, stock options or employee stock ownership plans (ESOP). *Dr. J. Robert Beyster,* founder and CEO of Science Applications International Corporation (SAIC), built an $8 billion employee-owned world-class research and engineering company on the principle that *"those who contribute to the company should own it, and ownership should be commensurate with employee contribution and performance as much as feasible."*

To engage the minds of everyone, you must ensure that your managers are following your stated values and are responsive to ideas and recommendations at the lowest levels. You can only do this if you are what *Dan Bannister,* former Chairman of DynCorp, calls a *"visible leader".* A visible leader is one who is consistently visible to the lowest and highest levels in the company and with the customer.

PROVIDE FOR PERSONAL GROWTH
To retain the best and brightest, it is essential that you create a *"learning organization"* that provides them with an opportunity to grow. Create an organization where learn-

ing is in the cultural bloodstream. A learning organization engenders a culture where there is an appetite for learning and ideas that can be translated into business solutions.

Establish career development counseling, formal training programs, and assign mentors to every individual. In addition, require self development outside the organization's formal programs. The commitment to personal growth by the individual is essential.

Elizabeth Hanford Dole, former President, American Red Cross is a prime example of how picking the best and establishing centers of excellence results in success. When Elizabeth Dole became President of the American Red Cross, she had already distinguished herself as a member of the Federal Trade Commission, as Secretary of Labor and as Secretary of Transportation.

She could have easily coasted through her tenure, but she chose to energize the venerable non-profit and in the process saved more than $140 million in annual operating costs in less than two years.

To accomplish this, she surrounded herself with talent. One of her first appointments was *William Reno* as Senior Vice President for Operations. Reno, a retired Army Three-Star General, has a reputation for getting things done. Mrs. Dole provided him with his marching orders and allowed him to succeed.

Reno identified contracting as a risk area (annual purchasing budget of more than $1.6 billion) and focused on establishing the American Red Cross' first professional contracting organization.

He, in turn, surrounded himself with talent and established a center of excellence. He brought in *Phil Yenrick*, a highly regarded former combat-veteran Army Colonel with a successful background in leadership, management, logistics and contracting, to head up this effort.

Yenrick assembled a team that included *Rob Kloak*, a very talented career Red Cross manager, and *Paul Dota*, another retired Army professional with a sterling reputation and extensive contracting experience.

Together, with active support from Dole and Reno, they achieved outstanding results – more than $140 million in annual savings and growing. They assembled a world-class team of contracting and purchasing professionals; trained more than 1,000 Red Cross personnel as field representatives for contracting and streamlined the procurement process nationwide for more than 30,000 full time American Red Cross professionals and hundreds of thousands of volunteers.

They have established a worldwide standard of contracting for nonprofit organizations. They practice the A*rt of the Possible*!

Dr. J. Robert Beyster, Founder, former Chairman & CEO, Science Applications International Corporation (SAIC) represents another great example of this best practice in the outstanding success enjoyed by Science Applications International. SAIC, prior to becoming a publicly-traded company, was the largest employee owned research and engineering firm in America with annual revenues in excess of $8 billion and more than 38,000 employees.

From the start, Dr. Beyster designed SAIC for "*professional people who want to perform superior scientific and technical work, who want to have a stake and a voice in the company's development and direction, and who expect fair rewards for doing excellent work.*"

SAIC has established centers of excellence in more than 150 cities worldwide. They have had more than 30 years of continued revenue and earnings growth. Dr Beyster credits the success of the company to its employee ownership.

"Someone who is involved with the company should own a piece of it," says Dr Beyster. *"Those who really perform well are rewarded by having their stock increased. People involved in the company should share in its success."*

He surrounded himself with talent and created centers of excellence. He practices the A*rt of the Possible*!

SUMMARY

Once you surround yourself with talent, you are well on your way to creating an organizational culture with no limitations. However, it requires constant attention at every level to ensure that your centers of excellence are effective.

Review and complete the **Art of the Possible Best Practice #2 SURROUND YOURSELF WITH TALENT** Self Assessment Checklist. Determine how you will reach "5's" for every requirement.

Your next task is to **Think Strategically** – *keep the big picture in perspective* throughout your organization.

Art of the Possible Best Practice #2
SURROUND YOURSELF WITH TALENT

CHECKLIST & PERSONAL ACTION PLAN SCORECARD

RATE HOW WELL YOU SURROUND YOURSELF WITH TALENT
(None - 0, High - 5)**

Focus Areas	Score	What Do You Need?	How Will You Do It?	When?
Value Principle & Energy Over Experience: 1. Hiring based on individual's demonstrated commitment to a principled work ethic first. 2. Energy and commitment to life and work valued over experience.				
Embrace Diversity: 1. Respect for people 2. No clones 3. No ethnic barriers 4. No gender barriers 5. Champions Teamwork				
Focus On Results – Demand Excellence: 1. Success defined & metrics established 2. People held accountable 3. 360° for Managers 4. Team & Individual Performance Agreements 5. Tools & resources provided				

Art of the Possible Best Practice #2
SURROUND YOURSELF WITH TALENT

CHECKLIST & PERSONAL ACTION
PLAN SCORECARD (Continued)

RATE HOW WELL YOU SURROUND YOURSELF WITH TALENT
(None - 0, High - 5)**

Focus Areas	Score	What Do You Need?	How Will You Do It?	When?
Identify & Build Leaders: 1. Leader Identification Process 2. Career Development Program 3. Leadership Training Program 4. Mentor Program				
Engage Every Mind – Make Them Stakeholders: 1. Every job is important 2. Team members empowered 3. Communications up & down 4. Visible leaders 5. "Using the brain of every worker" 6. Incentives (ESOP, Profit Sharing, etc.)				
Provide for Personal Growth: 1. Expose them to risk 2. Assign Mentors 3. Provide formal training opportunities 4. Require personal commitment to training				

Art of the Possible Best Practice #2
SURROUND YOURSELF WITH TALENT

CHECKLIST & PERSONAL ACTION
PLAN SCORECARD (Continued)

RATE HOW WELL YOU SURROUND YOURSELF WITH TALENT
(None - 0, High - 5)**

Focus Areas	Score	What Do You Need?	How Will You Do It?	When?
Scale: 0 – No Plan 1 – Thought about it 2 – Discussed it 3 – Partially Completed 4 – Articulated, Written, Validated 5 – Completed, Communicating & Practicing			**Your Action Plan to Achieve "5's" Across the Board**	

The Art of the Possible:
Create an Organization with No Limitations

1. GET FOCUSED
2. SURROUND YOURSELF WITH TALENT
3. THINK STRATEGICALLY
4. FORGE A HIGH-PERFORMANCE TEAM
5. MANAGE THE FUNDAMENTALS
6. MAINTAIN DISCIPLINE
7. COMMUNICATE

Art of the Possible Best Practice #3
THINK STRATEGICALLY

> *"When it comes to strategy, ponder less and do more."*
>
> *– Jack Welch, "Winning"*

Introduction	41
Institutionalize and Champion Strategic Thinking & Planning	42
Strategic Planning – The Process	43
Where are we now? A Checklist.	46
Where do we want (need) to be? A Checklist.	47
How do we get there? A Checklist.	48
Who will take us there? A Checklist.	49
How are we doing? A Checklist.	50
Strategic Plan Outline	52
Manage the Plan – A Strategic Model	53
Summary	53
Self-Assessment Checklist	55

INTRODUCTION

To practice the *Art of the Possible* you must foster a strategic mindset in your organization – *create a culture that values the big picture.* As global competitive pressures force businesses to become more responsive, effective organizational performance has become tied more closely to an organization-wide capacity for strategic thinking. No longer is such thinking only the province of those at the top or those charged with planning. Strategic thinking is a necessary component of everyone's job.

Strategic thinking focuses your entire organization on how to create a better future by being proactive. Strategic thinking always involves change. It requires you to change your present paradigms and your ways of thinking, relating, and performing. It is imagining the results you want to achieve in the future, it is practical dreaming . . . creating an ideal future by defining and achieving results that add value.

Strategic planning is the formal process of defining those requirements for delivering high performance results; for identifying what and how to get from your current realities to future ones that add value to your organization. It is not rigid or lock-step, but rather a self-correcting set of defining requirements and relationships for stating *What Is* in terms of results, and moving ever closer to *What Should Be* results and payoffs.

Strategic planning, as first articulated by C. Davis Fogg in *Team-Based Strategic Planning,* involves formally asking and answering five basic questions:

1. ***Where are we now?*** A comprehensive review and assessment, internal and external, of where you are as an organization, what resources and capabilities you now possess; an understanding of the current

marketplace and economic drivers impacting your performance.

2. **Where do we want (need) to be?** You must determine what is your preferred future to include the type of organization you want and performance metrics over time. Quite often, it isn't a matter of what you want, but a matter of what you need to be to remain competitive and viable. This provides the focus necessary for success.

3. **How do we get there?** Determine clear-cut choices about how to compete. You cannot be everything to everybody, no matter what the size of your business or how deep its pockets.

4. **Who must do what?** Internally assign responsibility for SMART goals and hold them accountable. Externally, identify and nurture those individuals and organizations that can be leveraged to help you attain your goals.

5. **How are we doing?** Establish methodologies for tracking performance metrics. Minimize meetings and reports.

The process of *strategic planning* integrates effective *strategic thinking* into a results oriented plan.

INSTITUTIONALIZE AND CHAMPION STRATEGIC THINKING AND PLANNING

Strategic planning is a management tool. As with any management tool, it is used to help an organization do a better job – to focus its energy, to ensure that members of the organization are working toward the same goals, to assess and adjust the organization's direction in response to a changing environment. In short, strategic planning is a disciplined effort to produce fundamental decisions and actions that shape and guide what an organization is, what it does, and why it does it, with a focus on the future.

Strategic planning is only useful if it supports strategic thinking and leads to *strategic management* - the basis for an effective organization. *Strategic thinking* means the entire organization continually asking, *"Are we doing the right thing?"*

Institutionalize Strategic Thinking and Planning

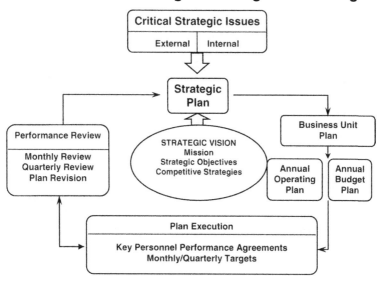

Ask and answer the five basic questions, articulate the answers in a comprehensive plan that sets forth SMART goals/objectives, assigns responsibility and accountability, provides the resources and continually measures performance. Communicate with the entire organization and get buy-in at every level. *You are practicing the Art of the Possible!*

STRATEGIC PLANNING – THE PROCESS

To practice the Art of the Possible, it is essential to utilize a comprehensive and disciplined approach to the strategic planning process.

Gather your key personnel and ask and answer the five basic questions. Utilize the checklists to prompt your thinking about the subject. If it isn't applicable, then move on to the next item. Write down the answers. You will find that as you progress through the questions it becomes apparent that it is a dynamic process and you will return to the previous question on several occasions to modify your responses.

STRATEGIC PLANNING

1. WHERE ARE WE NOW?
1. Internal/External Assessment
2. SWOT Analysis
3. Core Capabilities
4. Market Drivers

2. WHERE DO WE WANT/NEED TO BE?
1. Vision
2. Values
3. Mission
4. Value Proposition
5. SMART Goals
6. Metrics

3. HOW DO WE GET THERE?
1. Customers
2. Strategies
3. Programs
4. Priorities

5. HOW ARE WE DOING?
1. Monitoring
2. Consistency
3. Discipline
4. Reviews
5. Accountability

4. WHO WILL TAKE US THERE?
1. Key Personnel & Stakeholders
2. Most Effective Organization (MEO)
3. Leverage d Networks
4. Delegation/Accountability

ASK AND ANSWER FIVE BASIC QUESTIONS

Upon completion, you will have sufficient data to prepare a comprehensive Strategic Plan for your organization. You then turn planning into action by executing the plan. The purpose of the process is to prompt action in a focused and disciplined approach – *to practice the Art of the Possible.*

George Starke and Jack Lyon, Founders of Excel Institute, provides one of many success stories about organizations properly applying this best practice. One of the most heartening and encouraging is how George Starke, former NFL offensive lineman (Team Captain and Head Hog!) for the three-time Super Bowl Champion, Washington Redskins and Jack Lyon, Chairman Emeritus of PMI Parking in Washington, DC founded Excel Institute to provide automotive training for Washington, DC disadvantaged youth.

Upon retirement from the NFL, George Starke assumed a career as a new car dealer in Maryland. Living in the District of Columbia, he commuted to work each day and noted that too often many young people were standing on street corners and obviously not actively engaged in work; he also noted the climbing juvenile crime rate in DC.

Starke, a physics graduate of Columbia University, had a vision; he founded a non-profit organization, Excel Institute, with a single purpose – provide hope for the disadvantaged youth of DC. He personally provided the initial funding for the effort and asked his friend and mentor, Jack Lyon, then Chairman of PMI Parking, Inc., one of DC's largest parking management firms, to help him launch the Institute.

Excel Institute's success is now well documented and much of that success can be attributed to Starke and Lyon committing to development of a comprehensive strategic plan, executing that plan and monitoring its progress on a consistent basis.

Today, Excel Institute is debt-free, owns its own building, certified locally and nationally for training and education, and provides training to more than 200 youth annually. Excel Institute is sought after by other cities and states to replicate that effort. All of the above were strategic goals established in their Strategic Plan – they practice the Art of the Possible!

FIRST QUESTION - WHERE ARE WE NOW?

There are a number of key elements in the strategic planning process – none is more important than determining where you are currently. Baseline your strengths, weaknesses, opportunities and threats (the traditional SWOT analysis). This requires a candid and realistic look, internal and external, at your current world.

You must conduct a comprehensive review and assessment, internal and external, of where you are as an organization, what resources and capabilities you now possess; an understanding of the current marketplace, to include economic, social and political drivers impacting your performance.

Checklists:

External Assessment	Internal Assessment	Sources of Priority Strategic Issues

Areas for Opportunities and Threats:
• Markets/Customers
• Socio-demographics
• Competition
• Technology
• Economy
• Government/Political
• Geography
	Areas for strengths, weaknesses, and barriers to success:
	• Organizational
	  - Culture
	  - Structure
	  - Systems
	  - Processes
	  - People
	  - Management
	  - Practices
	• Financial Structure
	• Quality
	• Technology
	• Market Segments
	• Cost-Efficiency
	• Equipment
	• Facilities
	• Inventory
	• Asset Condition
	• Customer Service
	• Innovation
		• Strengths
		• Weaknesses
		• Opportunities
		• Threats

SECOND QUESTION - WHERE DO WE WANT (NEED) TO BE?

Once you have a clear understanding of where you are now, you are ready to determine where you want to be. Quite often, it is driven by where you need to be. You must orient your compass for achieving results.

Checklists:
Compass For Achieving Results

VISION	MISSION	VALUES
Your purpose in life. Where and what you want to be in the future: • Key numbers ($ sales, profit, locations, % wins, personnel, etc.) • Core markets (Priorities, Strengths, Not Saturated) • Core values • Strategic thrusts (Government, Commercial, International, IT, Services, etc.)	The arena of: • Products • Services • Customers • Technologies • Distribution Methods, and • Geography in which you'll compete to get results.	Desired attitudes and behavior toward internal and external stakeholders that will yield the culture and business results you want and that you will execute and turn into action through policy, programs, procedures, personnel selection.

It is critical that you establish SMART performance metrics that are focused. You have defined your vision and now must determine specific results over time that you have to attain to realize that vision. What gets measured gets done!

In defining your mission, you acknowledge that focus is the key. By identifying the products and services you can provide, you can then target specific customers who need them. Once you prioritize the customers, you can optimize your resources to focus on business development, marketing, delivering your products/services and customer service.

With your compass set, you are now ready to determine how you get will there. *You are practicing the Art of the Possible.*

THIRD QUESTION - HOW DO WE GET THERE?

Once again you develop internal and external strategies to meet your priority goals and objectives. Determine your overall financial strategies, establish priorities, determine the routes you will take to implement those strategies and be very clear about your value proposition (your competitive advantage).

Checklists:

Internal Strategies

OVERALL FINANCIAL STRATEGY	PRIORITIES	ROUTES	COMPETITVE ADVANTAGE
• Grow • Hold • Harvest • Get Out	• Markets • Business Units • Products • Services	• Acquire • Internal • Shut Down • Joint Venture • Divest • Restructure	• Cost • Value • Discriminator • Faster • Better • Cheaper

External Strategies

IDENTIFY/DEFINE YOUR CUSTOMERS
"One who values your product or service and who must be satisfied."
a. Who are your current customers?
b. Who could be your customers?
c. What do you do that is most valuable for your customers?
d. How do your customers define value?
e. How can you provide more value?
What is your Value Proposition?

External Strategies

CUSTOMER FOCUS Live Quality and Customer Service!	
• Product • Service • Distribution • Product Design • Quality • Value • Pricing	• Convenience • Image • Geography • Delivery • Reliability • Branding • Advertising/Promotion

FOURTH QUESTION - WHO MUST DO WHAT?

You have defined where you are in terms of resources and the marketplace, you have defined where you want to be, you have identified how you will get there and now you must determine who will do what to meet your goals. Assign specific responsibilities, provide resources and hold them accountable.

SAMPLE - STRATEGIC GOALS ASSIGNMENT CHART

Strategic Goals	Competitive Strategies (1-3 yrs.)	FY xxxx Actions	Resp.
1. Increase Company Revenue - $xxxx Annually by Fiscal year 20xx	*(1)* Increase sales to current Customer base	*DOD* *DOE* *EPA*	*Bob Orr*
	(2) Capture New Projects Worldwide	*China* *Japan* *Canada* *Former USSR*	*Tony Pasqual*
	(3) Capture New U.S. Projects	*Federal* *State* *Commercial*	*Jane Evers*

Internally, the priority now is to determine who in your organization has the ability to plan, organize and execute. Assignment of responsibility is pointless unless there is an understanding from the outset that resources will be provided to meet the goals and that the person responsible will be held accountable – there are consequences for success or failure.

Externally, identify organizations and personnel that you can leverage to meet your goals. Identify strategic partners who complement your capabilities or who provide products and services to your customers and/or prospective customers – personnel who know you and believe in your products and services.

FIFTH QUESTION - HOW ARE WE DOING?

You have established SMART goals that contain metrics – what gets measured gets done! It's time now to determine how you will monitor progress and maintain focus on the established goals while also maintaining the ability to adjust to change.

Hold quarterly meetings, as a minimum to review progress of assigned tasks and programs. Review individual goals and appraise performance. Ensure that there are rewards and consequences based on performance of teams and individuals. And finally, don't forget that most basic of leadership tools – MBWAR (management by walking around).

There are essentially three methods for monitoring progress:
1.   Meetings
2.   Reports
3.   Inspection

Balance is critical for this best practice. Don't overdo the meetings, reports and inspections. Determine how much coordination and oversight is needed to maintain focus and quality. The quote at the beginning of this best practice is appropriate; "*When it comes to strategy, ponder less and do more.*"

Work the plan and empower those key personnel with the responsibility and accountability to get the job done. Good planning mitigates the need for frequent internal meetings and reports and keeps the focus on the customer rather than internally trying to communicate through numerous meetings, reports and inspections.

Meetings – hold monthly or quarterly meetings with key personnel to review progress relative to the status of the strategic plan and annually, as a minimum, revisit the plan to adjust for change.

Ensure that for every meeting there is an agenda that clearly sets forth:
(1)   Purpose of the Meeting
(2)   Desired Outcomes
(3)   Specific Items to be discussed
(4)   Time lines for each item
(5)   Action Items for follow-on
(6)   Summary of meeting distributed to all attendees

Reports – minimize reports whenever possible, to include frequency of reports and details required. Once again, good planning should mitigate the need for lengthy and detailed reports – the focus should be on the customer, not internal non-essential documentation. Quality control mandates internal reporting, don't create additional ones.

Inspection – essential that you know what is going on. Go to the job sites, visit with the customers; let your personnel and your customer know that you are genuinely interested in delivering the very best product or services available. As Dan Bannister, Chairman/CEO of DynCorp says, *"Be a visible leader."*

However, onerous, labor intense and disruptive requirements for detailed inspections must be measured against the practical need for such information. Once again, good planning includes quality control and internal requirements should be met.

Bill Marriott, Chairman/CEO of Marriott Corporation, requires every executive to work in the housekeeping department of a hotel prior to assuming a key position in the company. It becomes obvious very quickly that quality requires oversight, but good planning and execution mitigates the need for unnecessary oversight.

STRATEGIC PLAN OUTLINE

1. **MEO:** Most Effective Organization, who will lead and be held accountable
2. **SMART Goals:** Quantity and quality (SMART), assigned responsibility and accountability
3. **Milestones:** Who, what, when, where (Critical Path – those events that take the longest)
4. **Resources:** Facilities, equipment, materials, data, subcontractors, people and organizations outside your control who must contribute and collaborate
5. **Risks:** Identify, quantify, mitigation plan
6. **Budget:** True costs to execute your plan

MANAGE THE PLAN – A STRATEGIC MODEL

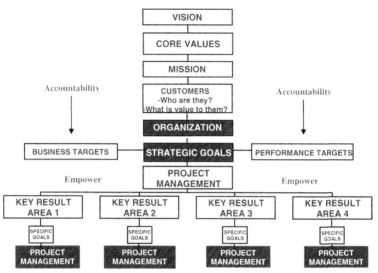

A STRATEGIC MODEL - APPLICATION OVERVIEW

SUMMARY

Each member of your entire organization is now focused on a better future and taking a proactive role, you have defined where you are now by evaluating your internal capabilities and resources and externally identifying where your products and services should be provided.

You have clearly defined where you want to be and established specific, measurable, attainable, relevant and trackable goals. You have defined your strategies for attaining those goals that tells you how you will get there and who will take you there. You have established metrics and methods for measuring progress. *You are practicing the Art of the Possible!*

Review and complete the **Art of the Possible Best Practice #3 THINK STRATEGICALLY** Self Assessment

Checklist. Determine how you will reach "5's" for every requirement.

Your next task is to **FORGE A HIGH PERFORMANCE TEAM** to execute your Strategic Plan.

Art of the Possible Best Practice #3
THINK STRATEGICALLY

CHECKLIST & PERSONAL ACTION PLAN SCORECARD

RATE HOW WELL YOU THINK STRATEGICALLY
(None - 0, High - 5)**

Focus Areas	Score	What Do You Need?	How Will You Do It?	When?
Institutionalize Strategic Thinking and Planning: 1. Mandate company requirement for annual plan. 2. Provide resources to facilitate process. 3. Mine entire organization for inputs. 4. Communicate throughout organization. 5. Champion Strategic Thinking!				
Question #1 – Where are we now? 1. Internal Assessment 2. External Assessment 3. Assumptions 4. Priority Issues 5. SWOT Analysis				
Question #2 – Where do we want to be? 1. Vision, Mission, Values 2. Products/Services 3. Customers 4. SMART Goals				

Art of the Possible Best Practice #3
THINK STRATEGICALLY

CHECKLIST & PERSONAL ACTION
PLAN SCORECARD (Continued)
RATE HOW WELL YOU THINK STRATEGICALLY
(None - 0, High - 5)**

Focus Areas	Score	What Do You Need?	How Will You Do It?	When?
Question #3 – How will we get there? 1. Financial Strategies 2. Priorities 3. Routes 4. Competitive Advantage (Value Proposition) 5. Customer Focus				
Question #4 – Who must do what? 1. Assign Responsibility, Provide Resources 2. Empower and Hold Accountable 3. Rewards and Consequences 4. Visible leaders 5. Leverage internal and external resources				

Question #5 – How are we doing?
 1. Quarterly Performance Reviews
   • Strategic Plan
   • Personnel
 2. Practical meetings scheduled
 3. Practical number and types of reports required
 4. Practical number and types of inspections				

Art of the Possible Best Practice #3
THINK STRATEGICALLY

CHECKLIST & PERSONAL ACTION
PLAN SCORECARD (Continued)
RATE HOW WELL YOU THINK STRATEGICALLY
(None - 0, High - 5)**

Focus Areas	Score	What Do You Need?	How Will You Do It?	When?
Scale: 0 – No Plan 1 – Thought about it 2 – Discussed it 3 – Partially Completed 4 – Articulated, Written, Validated 5 – Completed, Communicating & Practicing			**Your Action Plan to Achieve "5's" Across the Board**	

The Art of the Possible:
Create an Organization with No Limitations

1. GET FOCUSED
2. SURROUND YOURSELF WITH TALENT
3. THINK STRATEGICALLY
4. FORGE A HIGH-PERFORMANCE TEAM
5. MANAGE THE FUNDAMENTALS
6. MAINTAIN DISCIPLINE
7. COMMUNICATE

Art of the Possible Best Practice #4
FORGE A HIGH-PERFORMANCE TEAM

"Leadership is the quality that transforms good intentions into positive action; it turns a group of individuals into a team."

– T. Boone Pickens, Jr., Chairman
BP Capital Management

Introduction	63
What to require from every Team Member	64
What to require from every Team Leader	65
Exploiting the Potential – Recipe for Success	66
Stages in Team Development	67
The Most Effective Organization (MEO)	67
Fundamental Organizational Tasks – The Work Breakdown Structure	69
Win-Win Performance Agreements	70
Summary	73
Self-Assessment Checklist	75

INTRODUCTION

The phrase *"forge a high-performance team"* is used because *"forging"* is the term for shaping metal, a number of techniques are used which makes the metal easier to shape and less likely to fracture. This metaphor dramatically describes how critical your task is in shaping your organization so it does not fracture.

You have defined your vision, mission and values, surrounded yourself with talent, established centers of excellence, set your goals and developed strategies for achieving those goals. You are building your foundation for success. *You are practicing the Art of the Possible!*

You must now forge a high-performance team to execute your Strategic Plan. This best practice is about how you leverage the talents and capabilities of your team members. *High-performance teams consistently outperform peers in revenue growth, profitability and total return to shareholders.*

High-performance teams sustain superiority across time, business cycles, industry disruptions and changes in leadership. They ensure management processes and oversight practices provide the highest level of productivity and shareholder funds stewardship. They effectively balance current needs and future opportunities.

In performing work, there are *individual efforts and teams.* Efforts by individuals are never performed in a vacuum; what they do has an impact, internal and external. They are part of a team which achieves its purpose and goals through the combination of individual contributions.

The High-Performance Team

Each team member has the mission, values, and goals of the organization firmly ingrained in their day-to-day work ethic.
- Highly communicative group of people
- Team members with different backgrounds
- Skills and abilities that complement one another
- Team members are competent
- Team has a shared sense of mission
- Team has clearly identified goals
- Team is held accountable for results

A Team is an interdependent number of people with complementary skills who are committed to a common purpose, goals and working approach.

This best practice is about your entire organization becoming a high-performance team. High-performance Teams don't just happen, they must be deliberately built. High-performance team organizations practice *The Art of the Possible.*

WHAT TO REQUIRE FROM EVERY TEAM MEMBER

You have surrounded yourself with talent. You have selected personnel with a strong work ethic and principles and skills consistent with your vision, mission and values. To practice the *Art of the Possible* and forge a high performance team, ensure that each clearly understands that as a team member, they shall practice the following:

- **Commitment** -- created through involvement. They must demonstrate on a daily basis their commitment to the organizational goals.
- **Cooperation** -- share sense of mutual purpose. A Team is an interdependent number of people with complementary skills who are committed to a common purpose, goals and working approach.
- **Communication** -- strategic resource is information. Fact-based communication at every level is essential. Avoid rumor and innuendo.

- **Contribution** -- must carry own weight (coach problems and correct quickly or terminate-remove from team.). There is no room on a high-performance team for those who consistently demonstrate that they are not contributing.

WHAT TO REQUIRE FROM TEAM LEADERS

In today's workplace, the leader is a facilitator. Make it easy for your team to follow by setting the direction, sharing both the big picture and how the details fit in, having a disciplined approach and leading by example. The facilitative leader is a person who uses an interactive way of influencing people to achieve a shared vision. Require of each leader:

- **Highly developed interpersonal skills** -- team members need to belong, need personal recognition, need support. Set people up to win -- take heat with higher ups.
- **Organizational effectiveness** -- clear goals, values and expectations.
- **Share leadership with team members** -- develop your replacement.
- **Willingness to listen**
  - caring enough to ask
  - taking them seriously
  - dedicated enough to respond-implement their suggestions
  - express your appreciation for their input.
- **Pursuer of progress** -- continuously challenging everything.
- **Set expectation levels** -- expect more, get more!
- **Model expected behavior** -- walk it as you talk it.
- **Ability to deal quickly with the problem team members.**

Clearly define the role of the Team Leader:
- Keep the purpose, goals and approach relevant and meaningful
- Provide a specific, clear and compelling performance challenge to all team members
- Build commitment and confidence
- Strengthen the mix and level of skills
- Manage relationship with outsiders including removing obstacles
- Create opportunities for members
- Strike the right balance between action and patience in guiding the team to be in control of its destiny and performance

EXPLOITING THE POTENTIAL – A RECIPE

You have built a solid foundation for launching a high-performance team effort, essential to that effort and to exploit the potential of your team members you must ensure:

1. Clarity in goals.
2. Members selected based on skills and skill potential.
3. Clearly defined jobs and responsibilities.
4. Established ground rules.
5. Urgency in setting and seizing upon a few immediate performance oriented tasks and goals.
6. Beneficial team behaviors (friendship, concern and interest in others).
7. Clear communication.
8. Use of a disciplined approach.
9. Awareness of the group process.
10. Balanced participation.
11. Well defined decision-making procedures.
12. Exploit power of positive feedback, recognition and reward.
13. Team challenged regularly with fresh facts and information.

14.   Competent leadership.
15.   Accountability.

STAGES IN TEAM DEVELOPMENT

To practice *the Art of the Possible* will require an understanding of the evolution in the development of a high-performance team. In his book *The Team Handbook*, Peter Scholtes identified the five stages of developing a high-performance team:

Stage 1 - **Forming** – Getting the most qualified members on the team is difficult, but the leader must insist on the right people from the outset.

Stage 2 - **Storming** – Human nature dictates that personalities and agendas will clash, particularly if the leader has not set forth clear direction and does not hold people responsible and accountable.

Stage 3 - **Norming** – At some point, the personalities and agendas will become more compatible; when, is a function of leadership.

Stage 4 - **Performing** – The team comes together and becomes a high-performance team. At this stage, the leader must sustain superior performance.

Stage 5 - **Re-forming** – Quite often there are personnel turnover and the process begins again. Leadership must recognize this and take action.

Understanding this concept facilitates the leader's role in each stage of development.

THE MOST EFFECTIVE ORGANIZATION (MEO)

To form and forge a high-performance team, you must create the *most effective organization*, the MEO, from the outset. The MEO optimizes the number of personnel required to meet the mission and goals of the organization.

Industry standards provide a number of methodologies for determining the most effective organization. The most commonly used methodologies are zero-base analysis, benchmarking and, work-activity analysis.

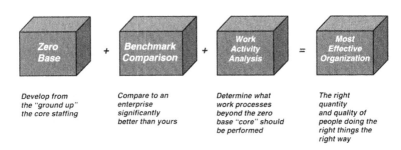

Zero Base	+	Benchmark Comparison	+	Work Activity Analysis	=	Most Effective Organization
Develop from the "ground up" the core staffing		Compare to an enterprise significantly better than yours		Determine what work processes beyond the zero base "core" should be performed		The right quantity and quality of people doing the right things the right way

Zero Base – Determine fundamental work requirements to meet your vision, values, mission and goals. Assume you have no personnel and ask the question *"What must be done?"* A work breakdown structure (WBS) facilitates this process. You will make a determination based on that analysis of *"Who will do what?"*

Benchmark Comparison – Compare your organization to other enterprises that are significantly better than yours. One of the best sources for that are professional associations such as the Professional Services Council (PSC) and others. Most often, a successful enterprise will operate with a significant number less than your Zero Base analysis inferred.

Work Activity Analysis – There are differences in work requirements and organizations. Determine what is different about your vision, mission and goals from other organizations performing comparable work. Baseline that comparability and delineate the differences. It then becomes a judgment call on the number of personnel needed to meet your specific goals.

You have used three proven methodologies to determine the right quantity and quality of people to do the right things the right way – you have created the Most Effective Organization (MEO). *You are practicing the Art of the Possible!*

FUNDAMENTAL ORGANIZATIONAL TASKS – THE WORK BREAKDOWN STRUCTURE (WBS)

To meet organizational mission requirements, there are fundamental tasks that must be performed. An effective tool to determine those tasks is to develop a work breakdown structure (WBS). The WBS is a breakdown of all of the requisite tasks needed to perform a specific function.

The WBS can be expressed in a linear progression (Gantt chart) or in a graphic format (Logic Tree). The graphic format is an effective communication tool because it shows relationships and provides the big picture. Also serves as an excellent gap analysis tool because you can visualize the tasks and determine what is missing.

The WBS is not the organization chart. *It asks and answers the fundamental question, "What must be done?" from which you determine "who must do what?"*

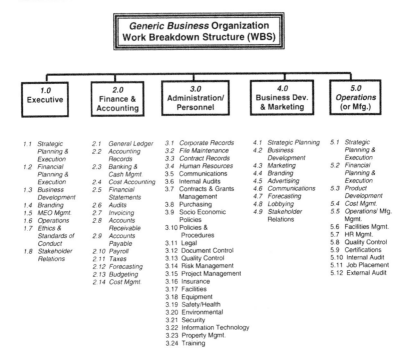

Generic Business Organization
Work Breakdown Structure (WBS)

1.0 Executive	2.0 Finance & Accounting	3.0 Administration/ Personnel	4.0 Business Dev. & Marketing	5.0 Operations (or Mfg.)

1.0
- 1.1 Strategic Planning & Execution
- 1.2 Financial Planning & Execution
- 1.3 Business Development
- 1.4 Branding
- 1.5 MEO Mgmt.
- 1.6 Operations
- 1.7 Ethics & Standards of Conduct
- 1.8 Stakeholder Relations

2.0
- 2.1 General Ledger
- 2.2 Accounting Records
- 2.3 Banking & Cash Mgmt.
- 2.4 Cost Accounting
- 2.5 Financial Statements
- 2.6 Audits
- 2.7 Invoicing
- 2.8 Accounts Receivable
- 2.9 Accounts Payable
- 2.10 Payroll
- 2.11 Taxes
- 2.12 Forecasting
- 2.13 Budgeting
- 2.14 Cost Mgmt.

3.0
- 3.1 Corporate Records
- 3.2 File Maintenance
- 3.3 Contract Records
- 3.4 Human Resources
- 3.5 Communications
- 3.6 Internal Audits
- 3.7 Contracts & Grants Management
- 3.8 Purchasing
- 3.9 Socio Economic Policies
- 3.10 Policies & Procedures
- 3.11 Legal
- 3.12 Document Control
- 3.13 Quality Control
- 3.14 Risk Management
- 3.15 Project Management
- 3.16 Insurance
- 3.17 Facilities
- 3.18 Equipment
- 3.19 Safety/Health
- 3.20 Environmental
- 3.21 Security
- 3.22 Information Technology
- 3.23 Property Mgmt.
- 3.24 Training

4.0
- 4.1 Strategic Planning
- 4.2 Business Development
- 4.3 Marketing
- 4.4 Branding
- 4.5 Advertising
- 4.6 Communications
- 4.7 Forecasting
- 4.8 Lobbying
- 4.9 Stakeholder Relations

5.0
- 5.1 Strategic Planning & Execution
- 5.2 Financial Planning & Execution
- 5.3 Product Development
- 5.4 Cost Mgmt.
- 5.5 Operations/ Mfg. Mgmt.
- 5.6 Facilities Mgmt.
- 5.7 HR Mgmt.
- 5.8 Quality Control
- 5.9 Certifications
- 5.10 Internal Audit
- 5.11 Job Placement
- 5.12 External Audit

WHAT MUST BE DONE?

Your organization's size, structure and make-up are a competitive advantage. When determining your team structure, explode out of your conventional thinking box. Question the core paradigms that guide or dictate the organization you have developed. The competition is doing more with less.

WIN-WIN PERFORMANCE AGREEMENTS

In all work there is the known and the unknown; the known is what is established in writing and clearly understood by the parties of the agreement. The unknown are expectations. Essential to creating a high-performance team is assuring that each team member is aware of their performance requirements and then provided the support and resources to meet those requirements.

EIGHT STEPS TO WIN-WIN PERFORMANCE AGREEMENTS

Step 1 - Determine the desired results
- *What is important*
- *Focus on contribution*
- *What is a win for all stakeholders*
- *Establish "SMART" Goals or Objectives*

Step 2 - Determine why the results are important
- *How do the desired results relate to the vision?*
- *Is there sufficient value-added and to whom?*
- *Is there adequate motivation to see the job through?*

Step 3 - Establish Guidelines
- *Boundaries*
- *Principles*
- *Policies*
- *Standardized Procedures*

Step 4 - Assess Resources
- *Human*
- *Technical*
- *Financial (Budget)*
- *Time (Schedule)*
- *Organizational (Training or Information Systems)*
- *External vs. Internal*

Step 5 - Baseline Accountability
- *Criteria or Standards for Measuring Performance*
- *What does success look like?*
- *What does failure look like?*

Step 6 - Identify Consequences and Opportunities
- *For Self (financial, career, etc....)*
- *For Organization*

- *For other Stakeholders*
- *What About a Risk Taken that didn't Work Out?*

Step 7 - Review Lessons Learned
- *Did the Agreement Help or Hinder the Process*
- *What Worked*
- *What Didn't Work*

Step 8 - Transition to Next Agreement
- *What is Next for the Individual and the Organization*
- *Start Framework on New Agreement*
- *How can Lessons Learned from Current Agreement be Applied to The Next Agreement*

By entering into a written win-win performance agreement with each team member, periodically reviewing that agreement and adjusting when necessary, you clearly define success.

Brent Armstrong, a former member of the Senior Executive Service (SES) for the Department of Energy and now Executive Vice President of Performance Results Corporation (PRC), personifies the facilitative leader and is one of the most adept leaders I know in building high performance teams.

His approach is straight forward: *"Treat your employees the way you would like to be treated, and they will respond. Accept the premise that your employees come to work wanting to do well at their jobs—it's up to you to create an environment in which they can, want to, and have the resources necessary to succeed!"*

Steve Perry, a young Army career officer, was given command of a dysfunctional organization with a critical national mission and resolutely turned it into a high-performance team. He determined very quickly that there was a lack of teamwork at every level; the root cause, lack of leadership and a clear understanding of vision, mission and values. He facilitated training and counseling for the team, promoted from within, removed the non-team players, dedicated resources and within months was leading a high performance team.

Charles Schwab, founder and Chairman of Charles Schwab & Co., Inc., built a high-performance team from scratch and sold his company in 1984 to Bank of America.

Unhappy with what he saw them doing with his company – they literally changed the character and culture – he bought the company back. Today, Charles Schwab & Co. is the largest discount brokerage firm ($300 billion) in the nation and a high performance team once again.

They all practice the Art of the Possible.

SUMMARY

To succeed, you are compelled to have an organization that is well led and peopled by principled and competent individuals that foster teamwork. To do otherwise, you place limitations on your organization and subsequently fail or do not realize your full potential. High-performance teams consistently outperform peers in revenue growth, profitability and total return to shareholders.

High-performance teams sustain superiority across time, business cycles, industry disruptions and changes in leadership. They ensure management processes and oversight practices provide the highest level of productivity and shareholder funds stewardship. They effectively balance current needs and future opportunities. High performance teams practice the Art of the Possible.

You have clearly defined where you want to be and established specific, measurable, attainable, relevant and trackable goals. You have defined your strategies for attaining those goals that tells you how you will get there and who will take you there. You have established metrics and methods for measuring progress. You have defined your Most Effective Organization (MEO) and are well on your way to forging a High Performance Team. *You are practicing the Art of the Possible!*

Review and complete the **Art of the Possible Best Practice #4 FORGE A HIGH PERFORMANCE TEAM** Self Assessment Checklist. Determine how you will reach "5's" for every requirement.

Your next task is to **MANAGE THE FUNDAMENTALS** and institutionalize processes and systems for a consistent approach to executing your Strategic Plan.

Art of the Possible Best Practice #4
FORGE A HIGH PERFORMANCE TEAM

CHECKLIST & PERSONAL ACTION PLAN SCORECARD

RATE HOW WELL YOU FORGE A HIGH PERFORMANCE TEAM
(None - 0, High - 5)**

Focus Areas	Score	What Do You Need?	How Will You Do It?	When?
Commitment to forge a High Performance Team!				
Mandate Team Member requirements: 1. Commitment 2. Cooperation 3. Communication 4. Contribution				
Mandate Team Leader requirements: 1. Highly developed interpersonal skills 2. Organizational effectiveness 3. Share leadership with team members 4. Willingness to listen 5. Pursuer of progress 6. Set expectation levels 7. Model expected behavior 8. Ability to deal quickly with problem team members				
Analyze Most Effective Organization (MEO) 1. Zero-Base Analysis 2. Benchmark Comparison 3. Work Driver Analysis				

Art of the Possible Best Practice #4
FORGE A HIGH PERFORMANCE TEAM

CHECKLIST & PERSONAL ACTION
PLAN SCORECARD (Continued)

RATE HOW WELL YOU FORGE A HIGH PERFORMANCE TEAM
(None - 0, High - 5)**

Focus Areas	Score	What Do You Need?	How Will You Do It?	When?
Develop Work Breakdown Structure (WBS) 1. Executive 2. Finance & Accounting 3. Administrative 4. Business Development & Marketing 5. Operations and/or Manufacturing				
Define Most Effective Organization (MEO) 1. Organization Chart 2. Assign Responsibility & Authority				
Win-Win Performance Agreements: Step 1 – Determine the desired results Step 2 – Determine why the results are important Step 3 – Establish Guidelines Step 4 – Assess Resources Step 5 – Baseline Accountability Step 6 – Identify Consequences & Opportunities				

Art of the Possible Best Practice #4
FORGE A HIGH PERFORMANCE TEAM

CHECKLIST & PERSONAL ACTION
PLAN SCORECARD (Continued)

RATE HOW WELL YOU FORGE A HIGH PERFORMANCE TEAM
(None - 0, High - 5)**

Focus Areas	Score	What Do You Need?	How Will You Do It?	When?
Step 7 – Review Lessons Learned Step 8 – Transition to next agreement				
Scale: 0 – No Plan 1 – Thought about it 2 – Discussed it 3 – Partially Completed 4 – Articulated, Written, Validated 5 – Completed, Communicating & Practicing		**Your Action Plan to Achieve "5's" Across the Board**		

1. GET FOCUSED
2. SURROUND YOURSELF WITH TALENT
3. THINK STRATEGICALLY
4. FORGE A HIGH-PERFORMANCE TEAM
5. MANAGE THE FUNDAMENTALS
6. MAINTAIN DISCIPLINE
7. COMMUNICATE

Art of the Possible Best Practice #5
MANAGE THE FUNDAMENTALS

> *"In turbulent times, you manage the fundamentals and you manage them well."*
>
> *– Peter Drucker*

Introduction	83
Identify Key Processes/Systems	84
Baseline Fundamental Processes and Conduct Continuous Process Improvement	85
Provide Effective and Practical Performance Support Tools	88
Utilize Integrated Teams for Process Development	90
Summary	93
Self-Assessment Checklist	94

MANAGE THE FUNDAMENTALS

INTRODUCTION

You have defined your vision, mission, and goals in a strategic plan, surrounded yourself with talent, formed the most effective organization, and are building a high performance team – clearly, you are practicing *the Art of the Possible!*

Critical to continued success is to emphasize to your organization the importance of sticking to the fundamentals, establishing standard systems and processes to support basic business functions, measuring their effectiveness and continually improving them – manage the fundamentals. It means sticking to the basics and using common sense and proven processes to approach complex problems.

As indicated in the work breakdown structure (WBS) you developed in determining your Most Effective Organization (MEO) in **Best Practice #4 – Forge a High Performance Team**, there are key functional requirements essential to business operations. The level of complexity and detail required varies with your business mission and your vision.

It is important that the basic systems and processes selected are compatible with your business focus and the level of complexity is compatible with your skill mix, internal and external. Many of your processes, such as accounting and quality are governed by industry standards and by customer requirements.

Processes must be documented with step by step procedures and baseline flow charts established for each. If there is no documentation defining and illustrating the process, then how can you be assured the process is followed on a consistent basis? How can you

improve the process if it isn't documented? Make no assumptions about processes.

This best practice is about how you organize, standardize and institutionalize the basic business functions in your organization to optimize day to day operations and profitability and to balance process with innovation and flexibility – to practice the *Art of the Possible*.

IDENTIFY KEY PROCESSES/SYSTEMS

Your generic WBS identifies, as a minimum, the following basic functions necessary in a business:

1. Executive
2. Accounting and Finance
3. Administrative/Personnel
4. Business Development and Marketing
5. Operations/Manufacturing

Within each of those primary functions, there are essential subtasks that are required to sustain the business/organization and to practice *the Art of the Possible*. Establish priorities and a plan to document each process so that they become an integral part of your daily operations. It isn't necessary to develop elaborate and cumbersome operation manuals; most will not be understood if they are not kept simple. Often a simple diagram and flow chart with standard document formats and checklists will suffice.

As a minimum, you need to establish standard policies and procedures for:

1. **Maintaining company records** such as legal documents, licenses, contracts and correspondence.
2. **Banking** (signature authority and records requirements) and **Finance** (line of credit).
3. **Accounting** (ledger, receivables/payables, payroll, taxes, tracking costs), estimating, invoicing and managing cash flow.

4. **Human resources** (MEO, hiring, terminations, career planning, training, benefits)
5. **Information technology**, operating systems, hardware and software.
6. **Planning, operations/manufacturing and project management**.
7. **Purchasing, contract administration and subcontract management.**
8. **Quality management:** Quality Control and Quality Assurance
9. **Business development**, forecasting, marketing, branding, proposal development, and customer relations.
10. **Risk Management**, safety, security and health.
11. **Ethics and Standards of Conduct, Communications**

BASELINE FUNDAMENTAL PROCESSES AND MAINTAIN CONTINUOUS PROCESS IMPROVEMENT

Once you baseline a process, your team can then continually work to improve it. For example, *cash flow* is the lifeblood of any business enterprise. There are a number of critical processes, when combined, directly impact the outcome. For example, a standard metric for managing that essential process is *Days Sales Outstanding (DSO)*.

DSO measures the number of days from the initial expenditure for a service or product until payment is received by the billing organization. The standard for DSO varies with industries and products. Obviously, the lower the number of days between expenditure and receipt of cash, the better the cash flow. Your DSO will be better with some customers than with others, depending upon the business and industry.

It is your responsibility to manage your cash flow. A consistent approach to a number of processes is essential to sustain a viable DSO:

1. **Estimating and Pricing** – Determining what your costs are, the price you will charge for the product or services and the terms and conditions for payment.
2. **Work/Task Management** – Assigning and tracking work.
3. **Project Management** – Initiating, planning, executing, controlling and closing out projects/work/tasks.
4. **Cost Accounting** – Tracking costs of work/tasks.
5. **Quality Control/Quality Assurance** – Cost effectively managing the work in accordance with the customer's requirements.
6. **Invoicing and Receipt of Payment** – Ensuring proper and timely invoices are submitted and follow-up for expeditious receipt of payments.
7. **Customer Relations Management** – Follow up with customer to ensure Satisfaction and manage potential for future opportunities.

Not properly documented, each of these processes can create a problem in cash flow. Properly baselined and documented, you can continually improve your cash flow over time, which goes directly to the bottom line.

Another example of the necessity for standardization of processes is how you grow your enterprise. Too often, business development does not begin with the end in mind and creates problems for the operations side or the ones who deliver the end product. Many organizations still operate on the premise that *"business development runs the bear on and operations has to skin it."* That paradigm has never worked very well.

By effectively standardizing the Business Growth process, your organization acknowledges that business growth is a continuum and that business development is a team effort from the outset and throughout the life-cycle of the engagement.

The business growth continuum begins with the end in mind, and a Business Growth Plan as part of the Strategic Plan. In Stage 1, **PLAN**, of the Continuum, the Business Growth plan confirms your value proposition and establishes SMART goals to meet financial targets.

In Stage 2, **IDENTIFY**, you identify those opportunities that will meet your goals and prioritize them as near-term, mid-term and long-term (you define those terms) goals. For each opportunity, you develop a Capture Plan (an aggressive, life-cycle approach to winning). In doing so, you establish a pipeline of opportunities that will perpetuate the enterprise. If you are a non-profit, identify sources of funds.

In Stage 3, **PURSUE**, you execute those Capture Plans. This is a team effort and you must manage customer relations at every level.

In Stage 4, **BID**, you pursue the opportunities and prepare offers to targeted customers. Many are in response to solicitations, others are unsolicited. Preparation of that offer, whether it is in the form of a formal proposal, a presentation or a simple price quote, is a team effort! Those who will perform the effort must be an integral part of the process.

Stage 5, **SUBMIT**, you negotiate the final agreement and enter into a contract. The contract sets forth the roles and responsibilities of the parties to the agreement and establishes the applicable law. You are legally and morally bound to perform in accordance with those terms and conditions.

Stage 6, **PERFORM**, you deliver what you said you would deliver in the contract. In all work there is the known and the unknown. The "known" is what is set forth in the agreement; the "unknown" are customer expectations. No one reads the contract.

You begin the cycle all over again to grow you current customers and to identify and capture new customers. Begin with the end in mind; it is a team effort.

PROVIDE EFFECTIVE AND PRACTICAL PERFORMANCE SUPPORT TOOLS

Develop a *"Toolbox"* for your organization that standardizes checklists, flow charts, proven approaches, best practices, software and other tools for consistent, effective and practical performance support. Indoctrinate and train all personnel in the application of the tools.

For example, when assigned a project, people too often jump right into the work without planning and thinking the effort through. The flow chart below facilitates getting started and planning and thinking through the life-cycle of a project:

GETTING STARTED - Begin with the End in Mind

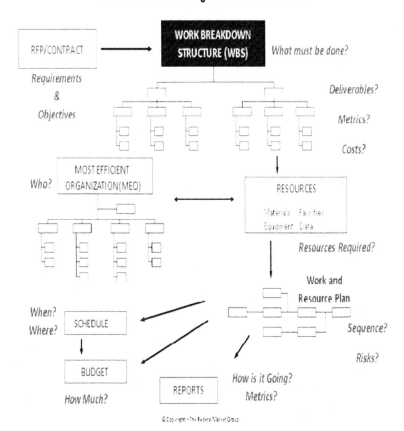

Checklists, such as Measures of Effectiveness Tables, developed by The Federal Market Group and based on best practices, facilitate evaluation of existing processes and systems:

Measures of Effectiveness Table

Critical Process Area: Finance, Accounting, Estimating

Principal Risk Areas	Measure of Effectiveness
1. Are there written policies and procedures in place and is there consistency in cost accounting?	a. Written policies and procedures. Approved accounting system b. Life-cycle cost accounting beginning with a Work Breakdown Structure (WBS) for each Program/Project with appropriate tracking numbers and system in place c. Total cost accounting
2. Are roles & responsibilities of finance, accounting and estimating personnel clearly defined/understood?	a. Organizational Charts with job descriptions b. Accountability
3. Is there an Earned Value Management System in place and functioning properly?	a. EVMS for every program/project b. All personnel trained on EVMS c. Customers trained on EVMS
4. Is there an established estimating process?	a. Accounting and Program/Project management integrated at task level b. Estimating process policies and procedures understood by all personnel c. Estimating process is life-cycle (from BD to Execution) d. Interface with Business Development
5. How do pricing analysts work with Business Development?	a. Pricing support integrated into business development function
6. Is there consistent Change-order accounting?	a. Scope Management procedures b. Documentation for all changes b. Number of Constructive Changes ratified c. Communication with PMs d. Interface with Contract Administration
7. How effective is cost management?	a. Cost controls, budget reviews b. Planning and Forecasting c. Procurement Planning d. Value Engineering
8. How effective is self-governance?	a. Internal audits b. External audits c. Ethics, fraud, waste, abuse monitoring

Data Sources:

UTILIZE INTEGRATED TEAMS FOR PROCESS DEVELOPMENT

For development or improvement of priority processes and systems, a proven approach is to charter an **Integrated Project Team (IPT)**. An IPT is a multi-functional, multi-organizational, interdependent group of people formed to capitalize on the strengths of all participants to meet the mission assigned to the team.

An IPT is a management technique that incorporates a systematic and consistent approach to the early integration and concurrent application of all the disciplines that play a part throughout a process or system's life cycle.

An IPT leads and integrates all activities necessary to deliver a Work Breakdown Structure (WBS) of all tasks required for the targeted process or system. A completed task is one that meets all the performance and operational goals of the specified functionality of that process or system.

IPT Process Map

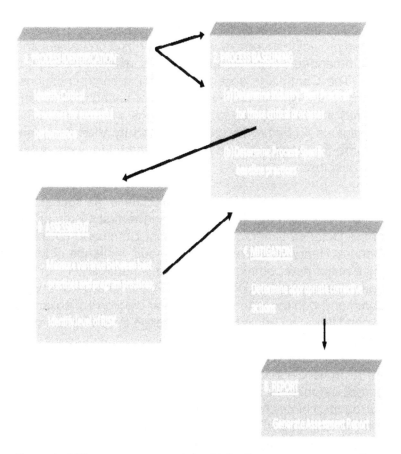

Beverly Milkman ran one of the U.S. Government's smallest executive agencies (19 full-time personnel), but one with a significant and challenging mission, The President's Committee for Purchasing from the Blind and Severely Disabled. She personifies the new breed of government leaders and has led award-winning changes at the Committee.

Part of the Committee's charter is to monitor and facilitate pricing for government sales by the National Industries for the Blind (NIB) and the National Industries for the Severely Handicapped (NISH). Facing more budget constraints, government agencies complained about the formula-based pricing of the NIB and NISH. Milkman assembled an integrated project team and reviewed the pricing processes and recommended a total paradigm shift to market-based pricing. The Committee accepted the IPT recommendations, changed the pricing process to market-based and subsequently increased sales to record highs while earning the prestigious *"Hammer Award"* presented by Vice President Al Gore for *"contributing to making government work better and cost less."*

Another fine example of this best practice is the success of *Army Major General Charles Henry,* the first Commander of the Defense Contract Management Command (DCMC). General Henry was given the enormous challenge of forming a major new command for contract management for the entire Department of Defense (DOD). In charge of a vast command with thousands of people and billions of dollars in expenditures, he applied common sense in solving complex problems.

As a proven leader, he focused on the mission from the outset, established the ground rules (his vision and values), surrounded himself with talented people (created Centers of Excellence), forged a high performance team, stuck to the basics and managed the fundamentals.

In his three years as Commander, DCMC became a model of government efficiency. Among the Command's accomplishments:
- Reduced or avoided $525 million in the cost of contract administration
- Reduced the number of people required for contract administration by 2,155

- Closed five intermediate headquarters and found jobs for virtually all displaced workers

He managed the fundamentals and he managed them well – he practices *the Art of the Possible.*

SUMMARY:

You have defined your vision, mission, and goals in a strategic plan, surrounded yourself with talent and formed the most effective organization. You are building a high performance team while managing the fundamentals – clearly, you are practicing *the Art of the Possible!*

*Review and complete the **Art of the Possible Best Practice #5 MANAGE THE FUNDAMENTALS** Self Assessment Checklist. Determine how you will reach "5's" for every requirement.*

Your next task is to **MAINTAIN DISCIPLINE** throughout the entire organization on a consistent basis.

Art of the Possible Best Practice #5
MANAGE THE FUNDAMENTALS

CHECKLIST & PERSONAL ACTION PLAN SCORECARD

RATE HOW WELL YOU WILL EMPHASIZE THE FUNDAMENTALS
(None - 0, High - 5)**

Focus Areas	Score	What Do You Need?	How Will You Do It?	When?
Identify Key Processes/ Systems 1. Executive 2. Accounting and Finance 3. Administrative 4. Business Development and Marketing 5. Operations/Manufacturing				
Baseline Fundamental Processes and Conduct Continuous Process Improvement 1. Maintaining company records 2. Banking and Finance 3. Accounting 4. Human Resources 5. Information Technology 6. Planning, Operations and Project Management. 7. Purchasing, Contract Administration and Subcontract Management. 8. Quality Management 9. Business Development				

Art of the Possible Best Practice #5
MANAGE THE FUNDAMENTALS

CHECKLIST & PERSONAL ACTION
PLAN SCORECARD (Continued)

RATE HOW WELL YOU WILL EMPHASIZE THE FUNDAMENTALS
(None - 0, High - 5)**

Focus Areas	Score	What Do You Need?	How Will You Do It?	When?
10. Risk Management 11. Ethics and Standards of Conduct 12. Communications				
Provide Effective and Practical Performance Support Tools 1. Process Flow Charts 2. Checklists 3. Best Practices 4. Standardized Software 5. Other				
Utilize Integrated Teams for Process Development 1. Process Identification 2. Process Baselining 3. Assessment 4. Mitigation 5. Reporting				
Scale: 0 – No Plan 1 – Thought about it 2 – Discussed it 3 – Partially Completed 4 – Articulated, Written, Validated 5 – Completed, Communicating & Practicing	**Your Action Plan to Achieve "5's" Across the Board**			

The Art of the Possible:
Create an Organization with No Limitations

1. GET FOCUSED
2. SURROUND YOURSELF WITH TALENT
3. THINK STRATEGICALLY
4. FORGE A HIGH-PERFORMANCE TEAM
5. MANAGE THE FUNDAMENTALS
6. MAINTAIN DISCIPLINE
7. COMMUNICATE

Art of the Possible Best Practice #6
MAINTAIN DISCIPLINE

"The good-to-great companies built a consistent system with clear constraints, but they also gave people freedom and responsibility within the framework of that system. They hired self-disciplined people who didn't need to be managed, and then managed the system, not the people."

– Good To Great by Jim Collins

Introduction	101
Deliver Quality Every Day – Create a Community of Practice	102
The Business Case for Project Management	104
Role of the Project Manager	107
Six Step Approach to Create a Community of Practice	108
Summary	110
Self-Assessment Checklist	112

INTRODUCTION

You have defined your vision, mission, and goals in a strategic plan, surrounded yourself with talent, formed the most effective organization and assigned responsibility to execute the plan. You are building a high performance team and managing the fundamentals – you are practicing the *Art of the Possible*.

Your compass is pointing to success! Now, your challenge is to maintain the progress you achieve over a sustained period and on a consistent basis. *You must maintain discipline.* In its most general sense, *discipline* refers to systematic instruction given to a disciple. This sense also preserves the origin of the word, which is Latin *disciplina*, "instruction." It is also defined as an *"orderly or prescribed conduct or pattern of behavior."*

This best practice is about how you create a **Community of Practice** in your organization that focuses on the consistent application of proven systems and processes that support superior performance. It is about how you train and indoctrinate your Team to ensure that processes, systems and common sense are applied on a consistent basis every time.

Jim Collins' Good to Great is a definitive study of companies that far exceeded their competition in performance over a sustained period of time and the common attributes found in those organizations. In the study, Collins sets forth that in every company that transitioned from being a good company to a great company, there was a "culture of discipline" – disciplined people, disciplined thought and disciplined action.

His findings are spot-on. If you do not have a "culture of discipline" in your organization, you are at risk. It comes in many forms. GE created *"Six-Sigma",* Hewlett Packard created *"The HP Way"*, Boeing adopted *"Lean Thinking"*, and there are many others. Creating a *Community of Practice* where team members are focused on superior performance specific to your organization will serve the same purpose. You will practice the *Art of the Possible*.

DELIVER QUALITY EVERY DAY – CREATE A COMMUNITY OF PRACTICE

Community is defined as *"friendly association, fellowship."* **Practice** is defined as *"to put knowledge into practice; work at or follow a profession."* Creating your own **Community of Practice** focuses your organization on performance.

You need to create an opportunity for personnel to continually improve their skills by sharing best practices and lessons learned. Provide an environment that promotes collegiality and pride in the ethics, knowledge, skills, recognition and rewards of being a professional in your organization. It is the framework for what Collins refers to as a "culture of discipline."

As discussed in **Art of the Possible Best Practice #5 - Manage the Fundamentals**, you must establish standard processes and systems and institutionalize those standards for your organization. Ensure that all your personnel are trained and skilled in the application of those standards. Your *Community of Practice* facilitates the daily application of those standards and processes. *They are disciplined.*

All work performed by organizations typically fall into one of two categories, operations or projects. The primary differences between operations and projects are that operations are ongoing and repetitive, projects are temporary and unique (tasks, delivery orders, contracts, programs). The common characteristics of operations and projects are that the work activity is usually resource constrained, performed by people, planned, executed and controlled.

A proven organizational approach to managing day to day ongoing operations as well as tasks, delivery orders, contracts and other projects is *Project Management*. **Project Management is the application of knowledge, skills tools, and techniques to organizational activities in order to meet or exceed stakeholder needs and expectations.**

Meeting or exceeding stakeholder needs and expectations invariably involves balancing competing demands among scope, time, cost and quality, stakeholders with differing needs and expectations, identified requirements (needs) and unidentified requirements (expectations).

The rigors and discipline of Project Management provide your organization a common framework for the application of your standard processes and systems. It is also an international standard. It contains an internationally accepted common lexicon and glossary of terms and definitions. It is the catalyst that brings together the languages of technology and business; both internal and external to your organization.

The **Project Management Body of Knowledge (PMBOK™)** contains nine specific areas of knowledge and skills necessary for successful performance of work. It also requires the consistent application of five processes in performing that work. PMBOK is an international standard maintained by the Project Management Institute (PMI). Worldwide membership in PMI exceeds 250,000 professionals who continuously share best practices. (www.pmi.org)

Create a *Community of Practice* in your organization and you will facilitate the consistent application of the nine knowledge and skill areas and the five processes in all work performed as well as the consistent application of your standard processes and systems. You will practice the *Art of the Possible.*

THE BUSINESS CASE FOR PROJECT MANAGEMENT

Project Management consists of directing, coordinating and facilitating the optimal use of human and material resources throughout the life of an asset or project to achieve predetermined objectives of scope, quality, time, costs and customer satisfaction. ***Operations Management*** consists of overseeing day to day activities required to operate, maintain and repair assets which provide services to a customer. The rigors and discipline of Project Management are applicable to both.

PMBOK contains nine specific functional areas that require knowledge and skill in all work to be performed. When applied on a consistent basis, there is a higher probability of successful completion of work on time and within budget.

The numbers (4-12) represent the corresponding chapters in the PMI PMBOK Manual.

The discipline of project management requires the execution of five processes during the life-cycle of a task, project, or ongoing activity. Institutionalizing those processes in your organization provides a framework that ensures a higher probability of success.

1. ***Initiating Processes*** - recognizing that a task, project or phase should begin and committing to do so.
2. ***Planning Processes*** - devising and maintaining a workable scheme to accomplish the business need that the project or task was undertaken to address.
3. ***Executing Processes*** - coordinating people and other resources to carry out the plan.
4. ***Controlling Processes*** - ensuring that project objectives are met by monitoring and measuring progress and taking corrective action when necessary.
5. ***Closing Processes*** - formalizing acceptance of the project or task and bringing it to an orderly end.

Project Management Processes

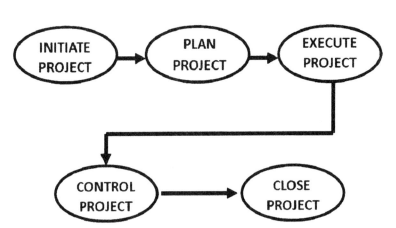

Make it easy for your personnel to get their work done. Ensure that you have the processes, systems and tools in place to support their efforts. Monitor and measure progress, take corrective action when necessary, reward success. Coach failure and encourage improvement.

Common themes in successful organizations that practice project management:

- Have a clear <u>direction</u>
- <u>Communicate</u> with all the players
- Consistently make the <u>best decision</u>
- Complete <u>planning</u> before doing
- <u>Identify Risks</u> up front
- Flawlessly <u>execute</u> the plan
- <u>Align & motivate</u> the team

Your *Community of Practice* embraces discipline and should provide significant results:

1. Zero incidents in Safety and Environmental performance
2. Full compliance with all applicable laws & regulatory requirements
3. Meet all contract/customer requirements
4. Faster cycle time
5. Lower cost
6. Successful operability
7. All business activities conducted with honesty, integrity & professionalism

ROLE OF THE LEADER

In creating the Community of Practice and the culture of discipline, the leader must ensure:

1. Required quality/job performance is provided to the customer.
2. Best practices are being properly used on all work.
3. Timely and complete communication among all key stakeholders.
4. You consistently make the right decisions.
5. A sound project execution plan is in place and actual execution follows the plan.
6. Risks are properly assessed/analyzed/mitigated.
7. Team synergy exists and is leveraged.
8. Information on project status is accurate, timely and unbiased

9.   Cost estimates and schedules are realistic and contain adequate contingencies.
10. Contractors and suppliers deliver.
11. Competitive advantage for the organization is gained through its' performance.
12. Integrity and Standards of Conduct are maintained.

SIX STEP APPROACH TO CREATE A COMMUNITY OF PRACTICE

A Six-Step Approach to institutionalize a Program/Project Management Community of Practice in your organization.

SIX-STEP APPROACH

STEP 1
   PMBOK Standard
STEP 2
   Certification Program
STEP 3
   PM Training
STEP 4
   Community of Practice
STEP 5
   Mentoring Program & Succession Plan
STEP 6
   Performance Metrics and Accountability

STEP 1 – Select the Project Management Body of Knowledge (PMBOK) as an organization standard. PMBOK provides the framework for discipline. The nine functional skill and knowledge areas and the five processes establish a common language and consistent approach to all work in your organization.

STEP 2 – Establish an internal certification program as a standard for career development and for advancement. The certification should be mandatory and include every level of management in the organization. Externally, PMI offers the Project Management Professional (PMP) certification. Your certification program provides both your Team and your customers a strong message about your commitment to quality and performance excellence.

STEP 3 – Establish a program to train all personnel in PMBOK and the five processes. Vary the training levels to accommodate entry level, mid-level and advanced personnel requirements. Use the training to develop your leaders internally and to maintain a pipeline for leadership positions due to growth.

STEP 4 – Identify Mentors for new hires and personnel identified as future leaders. Train the Mentors and monitor their efforts. Establish Individual Development Plans (IDP) for key personnel. Establish and maintain a Succession Plan for every key position in the organization.

STEP 5 – Create a Community of Practice webpage to facilitate communications about performance. Encourage the exchange of best practices and new ideas and approaches. Provide a summary of each product, program/project, business unit or activity of your organization so that all personnel know the organizational capabilities. As you grow, establish an internal Board of Advisors of certified project managers to review the activities of the Community of Practice and recommend best practices.

STEP 6 – Establish performance agreements and metrics for all personnel and hold people accountable at every level. Reward success, council and coach failure.

Ben Medley provides an excellent example of practicing the *Art of the Possible.* Medley, as President of Computer Sciences Corporation's Applied Technology Division (CSC/ATD), was hired to lead an already successful organization. He was not satisfied with the status quo. He acknowledged that he had a good organization, but he wanted a great organization and set out to accomplish that task.

He immediately began the Strategic Planning process and gathered his key personnel to ask and answer the five basic questions. Upon completion of the plan, he set out to create a *Community of Practice* for his team with the value proposition *"The Best for The Best."* He implemented the Six Step Process to institutionalize Project Management, PMBOK, as the performance standard for his TEAM.

Medley mandated that all direct reports to him and each of their direct reports must meet internal project management certification. Direct reports to him had one year, their direct reports had two years to become certified or elect to leave the team. He created an intranet website for the organization to monitor progress and share best practices. Within two years, he doubled his operating income, increased the award-fee average on his government contracts from 84% to 94% and closed more than $12 billion dollars in new business.

He mandated discipline and he met or exceeded all of his goals – he practices the *Art of the Possible!*

SUMMARY
You have defined your vision, mission, and goals in a strategic plan, surrounded yourself with talent, formed the most effective organization and assigned responsibility to execute the plan. You are building a high performance team and

managing the fundamentals. You have mandated discipline and created a Community of Practice as the framework for your culture of discipline – you are practicing the *Art of the Possible*.

Review and complete the **Art of the Possible Best Practice #6 MAINTAIN DISCIPLINE** *Self Assessment Checklist. Determine how you will reach "5's" for every requirement.*

Your next task is to **COMMUNICATE** throughout the entire organization and with your customers on a consistent basis.

Art of the Possible Best Practice #6
MAINTAIN DISCIPLINE

CHECKLIST & PERSONAL ACTION PLAN SCORECARD

RATE HOW WELL YOU WILL MAINTAIN DISCIPLINE
(None - 0, High - 5)**

Focus Areas	Score	What Do You Need?	How Will You Do It?	When?
Commit to a culture of discipline and to creating a Community of Practice.				
Implement Six Step Approach to Create a Community of Practice Step 1 – Establish PMBOK as Standard 1. Project/Task Initiation Management 2. Scope Management 3. Time and Schedule Management 4. Cost Management 5. Quality Management 6. Human Resources Management 7. Communications Management 8. Risk Management 9. Procurement Management				
Institutionalize five processes: 1. Initiating Processes 2. Planning Processes 3. Executing Processes				

Art of the Possible Best Practice #6
MAINTAIN DISCIPLINE

CHECKLIST & PERSONAL ACTION PLAN SCORECARD (Continued)

RATE HOW WELL YOU WILL MAINTAIN DISCIPLINE
(None - 0, High - 5)**

Focus Areas	Score	What Do You Need?	How Will You Do It?	When?
4. Controlling Processes 5. Closing Processes				
Step 2 – Establish Certification Program				
Step 3 – Train Personnel				
Step 4 – Establish Community of Practice and Communicate				
Step 5 – Establish Mentoring and Succession Planning				
Step 6 – Establish Performance Metrics and hold Personnel accountable				
Scale: 0 – No Plan 1 – Thought about it 2 – Discussed it 3 – Partially Completed 4 – Articulated, Written, Validated 5 – Completed, Communicating & Practicing	**Your Action Plan to Achieve "5's" Across the Board**			

The Art of the Possible:
Create an Organization with No Limitations

1. GET FOCUSED
2. SURROUND YOURSELF WITH TALENT
3. THINK STRATEGICALLY
4. FORGE A HIGH-PERFORMANCE TEAM
5. MANAGE THE FUNDAMENTALS
6. MAINTAIN DISCIPLINE
7. COMMUNICATE

Art of the Possible Best Practice #7
COMMUNICATE!

> *"At the root of most communications problems are perceptions or credibility problems. None of us see the world as it is but as we are. . ."*
>
> – *Stephen R. Covey,* Principle-Centered Leadership

Introduction	119
Communications Planning	121
Information Distribution	122
Performance Distribution	123
Manage Stakeholders	124
Summary	126
Self-Assessment Checklist	127

COMMUNICATE!

INTRODUCTION

You have defined your vision, mission and goals in a strategic plan, surrounded yourself with talent, formed the most effective organization and assigned responsibility to execute the plan. You are building a high performance team, managing the fundamentals and creating a Community of Practice to sustain superior performance – you are practicing the *Art of the Possible.*

Now, you must generate and manage information. You must **communicate** your vision, values, mission, commitment to quality and superior performance, and change, internally and externally, to your Team, customers and potential customers. Communications is a powerful tool that can make a vital contribution to organizational success.

Good communications enables you to build lasting relationships with your target audiences, transform difficult relationships and avert misunderstanding that leads to ill will. *Poor communications* leaves your Team members and customers feeling ignored, and reluctant to want to stay with you or do business with you again.

Communications is a two-way process. As well as communicating internally and externally your message, your organization must also establish mechanisms to receive information. Continually assess the effectiveness of all of your communication processes, tools and techniques.

In the rigors and discipline of Project Management, Communications Management is one of the nine critical functional skills and knowledge areas required. It employs the processes necessary to ensure timely and appropriate generation, collection, distribution, storage, retrieval and ultimate disposition of organizational information.

Identifying the informational needs of the stakeholders and determining a suitable means of meeting those needs is an important factor for organizational success. ***Communications Management processes include Communications Planning, Information Distribution, Performance Reporting and Managing Stakeholders.*** Develop a comprehensive **Communications Management Plan** to institutionalize these processes in your organization and you will practice the *Art of the Possible.*

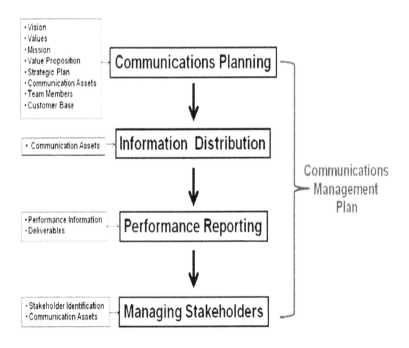

Communications Management Process

COMMUNICATIONS PLANNING

Communications planning determines the information and communications needs of the organization stakeholders. For example, who needs what information, when will they need it, how will it be given to them, and by whom. The information needs and methods of distribution will vary widely. The communications plan should be reviewed continuously and revised as needed to ensure continued applicability. To practice the *Art of the Possible*, you must identify communications requirements in terms of **Input, Tools and Techniques, and Outputs**.

- **INPUTS** – Consider such factors as:
  1. **Organization Factors** that include vision, values, mission, organizational structure (the MEO), value proposition, processes and systems in place, best practices, lessons learned and others. Requires stakeholder analysis.
  2. **Communication Assets** includes organizational processes and systems that manage your documentation, reporting requirements, website, meetings, lessons learned, historical data, website, intranet, mailing lists and other information.
  3. **Strategic Plan** that contains information about external drivers such as your market and its political and economic environment, your marketing and branding plans, goals and strategies, Team members assigned responsibility and external personnel that you must leverage to meet your goals. Includes constraints and assumptions.
  4. **Customer Base** must include current and potential customers and an external stakeholder analysis.

- **TOOLS AND TECHNIQUES** – Consider such factors as:
  1. **Requirements Analysis** includes determining the type and format of needed with an analysis of the

value of that information. Organization assets and resources are expended only on information that contributes to success, or where a lack of information can lead to failure.

2. **Communications Technology** includes the methodologies used to transfer information among organizational stakeholders. Such as: the urgency of the need for information, the availability of technology, the expected staffing, the length of the requirement and the organizational environment.

- **OUTPUTS – COMMUNICATIONS MANAGEMENT PLAN**
  1. **Communication Item.** The information that will be distributed.
  2. **Purpose.** The reason for the distribution of the information.
  3. **Frequency.** How often the information will be distributed.
  4. **Start/End Dates.** The timeframe for the distribution of the information.
  5. **Format/Medium.** The layout of the information and the method of transmission.
  6. **Responsibility.** The Team member charged with the distribution of the information.

INFORMATION DISTRIBUTION

Information Distribution involves making information available to project stakeholders in a timely manner. It includes implementing the communications management plan, as well as responding to unexpected requests for information.

1. **Communications Skills** – The sender is responsible for making the information clear and complete so the receiver can receive it correctly and for confirming that it is properly understood.
   - Written and oral, listening and speaking

- Internal and external
- Formal or informal
- Vertical and horizontal

2. **Information Gathering and Retrieval Systems** – Information can be gathered and retrieved through a variety of media including manual filing systems, electronic databases, management software and systems that allow access to technical documentation and other types of information.

3. **Information Distribution Methods** – Information collection, sharing, and distribution to stakeholders in a timely manner. Information distribution can be distributed using a variety of methods:
    - Meetings, hard-copy document distribution, manual filing systems, and shared access electronic databases.
    - Electronic communication and conferencing tools, e-mail, fax, voice mail, telephone, video and Web conferencing.
    - Electronic tools, Web interfaces, management software, meeting and virtual office support software, electronic dashboards, portals and collaborative management tools.
    - Lessons Learned, project/task records, reports, presentations, feedback from stakeholders and stakeholder notifications.

PERFORMANCE REPORTING
The performance reporting process involves the collection of all baseline data, and distribution of performance information to stakeholders. Generally this performance information includes how resources are being used to achieve goals and objectives on projects or tasks and addresses:

1. Scope
2. Schedule
3. Quality

4. Cost
5. Risk

Performance Reports include:
1. Work Status
2. Performance Measurements
3. Completion Forecasts
4. Quality Control/Assurance
5. Changes
6. Deliverables
7. Recommended Corrective Actions
8. Process and systems updates

MANAGE STAKEHOLDERS

Stakeholder management refers to managing communications to satisfy the needs of and resolve issues with stakeholders. Actively managing communications with stakeholders increases the likelihood that you will succeed. The methods of communications identified for each stakeholder in the communications management plan are utilized during stakeholder management.

1. **Communication Methods** – Face-to-face meetings are the most effective means for communicating and resolving issues, however, when not warranted or practical, telephone calls, electronic mail, and other electronic tools are useful for exchanging information and dialogue.

2. **Internal Communications** – Establish a Community of Practice with scheduled meetings, intranet webpage, off-site meetings, sharing best practices, incentives, company on-line newsletters.

3. **External Communications** – Be proactive and periodically share with customers good news about your organization. Visit the customer just to say thank you. Mandate a Communications Plan for each business unit or program/project.

4. **Action-Item Log** – Tool used to document and monitor resolution of issues. Be proactive, anticipate issues and assign resolution to a variety of Team members.

An example of how not to manage communications was recently demonstrated when a client of The Federal Market Group (FMG) lost a major contract re-compete after fourteen years on the job. FMG was retained to provide an independent evaluation of the client's performance on a large multi-year government contract three months prior to the submission of a proposal. The client was the incumbent contractor for the previous 14 years.

FMG's methodology includes reading and understanding the requirements of the contract, focusing on critical internal systems and processes, and the client's program management plan, then evaluating them using Methods of Effectiveness Tables based on industry best practices. FMG focuses on both strengths and weaknesses and weigh the results in terms of High, Moderate or Low Risk. Solutions are recommended for each risk area.

One phase of the process includes interviews of the client's customers with a client executive present. FMG asks only two questions. The first question is *"Can you share with us any concerns you have with the Contractor's performance?"* The second question is *"Can you elaborate on those concerns?"*

The answers varied with each interview and a pattern emerged that was inconsistent with the client's perception of their image with the customer. Consistently, comments from the customer indicated that although the client had a reasonable performance record, there seemed to be serious problems with their union relations and the problems were perceived as long-running and unsolvable.

FMG's audit of critical internal processes and systems indicated they did not have a Communications Plan for this major program. The client attempted to correct the perception, but it was too late. The irony of this is that the relations with the unions had been addressed a year earlier and they had entered into a full partnership to create a high-performance team and the union supported the contractor's re-compete.

Sadly, that information had never been communicated in a timely manner to the customer at the local level and to the higher commands that had the same negative perceptions. In the debrief informing the contractor why they lost, that perception was cited as one of the major factors in not selecting them to continue.

"At the root of most communications problems are perceptions or credibility problems. None of us see the world as it is but as we are. . ."

SUMMARY
Identifying the informational needs of the stakeholders and determining a suitable means of meeting those needs is an important factor for organizational success. Build a *High Performance Team*, create a *Community of Practice* and develop a comprehensive **Communications Management Plan** to institutionalize proactive communications in your organization and you will practice the *Art of the Possible.*

*Review and complete the **Art of the Possible Best Practice #7s COMMUNICATE!** Self Assessment Checklist. Determine how you will reach "5's" for every requirement.*

Art of the Possible Best Practice #7
COMMUNICATE!

CHECKLIST & PERSONAL ACTION PLAN SCORECARD

RATE HOW WELL YOU WILL COMMUNICATE!
(None - 0, High - 5)**

Focus Areas	Score	What Do You?	How Will You Do It?	When?
Commit to a Com-munications Plan for Your Organization: *1. Communications Planning* *2. Information Distribu-tion* *3. Performance Report-ing* *4. Manage Stakeholders*				
Communications Planning: 1. Inputs 2. Tools and Techniques 3. Outputs				
Information Distribu-tion: 1. Communications Skills 2. Information Gather-ing and Retrieval Systems 3. Information Distribu-tion Methods				
Performance Report-ing: 1. Scope 2. Schedule 3. Quality 4. Cost 5. Risk				

Art of the Possible Best Practice #7
COMMUNICATE!

CHECKLIST & PERSONAL ACTION
PLAN SCORECARD (Continued)

RATE HOW WELL YOU WILL COMMUNICATE!
(None - 0, High - 5)**

Focus Areas	Score	What Do You?	How Will You Do It?	When?
Manage Stakeholders: 1. Communications Methods 2. Internal Communications 3. External Communications 4. Action-Item Log				
Scale: 0 – No Plan 1 – Thought about it 2 – Discussed it 3 – Partially Completed 4 – Articulated, Written, Validated 5 – Completed, Communicating & Practicing			**Your Action Plan to Achieve "5's" Across the Board**	

CONCLUSION

"I am not remotely interested in just being good."

- Vince Lombardi

As stated at the outset, this book is about creating an organization where things get done, where anything is possible. This book is about excellence and success!

To succeed, you are compelled to have an organization that is well led and peopled by principled and competent individuals that foster teamwork. To do otherwise, you place limitations on your organization and subsequently fail or do not realize your full potential.

This book represents an integrated leadership and management process that provides the reader with a proven and practical approach to success. It focuses on the positive – on what works. It is practicing _the art of the possible; creating an organizational culture that knows no limitations._

The guidelines provided will clearly facilitate your efforts to get focused, surround yourself with talent, think strategically, forge a high performance team, manage the fundamentals, maintain discipline and to communicate effectively.

Nothing will happen, however, until you, as the leader, make a genuine commitment to lead. You are the catalyst. You must take responsibility for making things happen. That is the first step to practicing the Art of the Possible and creating an organization with no limitations.

Lead, follow or get out of the way!

BIBLIOGRAPHY

Bartlett, John, *Bartlett's Familiar Quotations*, 17th Edition, Little Brown, 2008

Beyster, Robert J., et.al, The SAIC Solution, John Wiley & Sons, 2007

Collins, Jim, *Good to Great*, Harper Business, 2001

Covey, Stephen R., *Principle-Centered Leadership*, Free Press, 1990

Drucker, Peter F., *Managing in Turbulent Times*, Harper & Row, 1980

Drucker, Peter F., *The New Realities*, Harper & Row, 1989

Drucker, Peter F., *Management Challenges for the 21st Century*, Harper Business, 1999

Fisher, Roger and Ury, William, *Getting to Yes*, 2nd Edition, Penguin Press, 1981

Fogg, C. Davis, *Team-Based Strategic Planning*, AMACOM, 1994

Gates, Bill, et.al, *The Road Ahead*, Viking, 1995

Goleman, Daniel, *Emotional Intelligence*, Bantam, 1995

Charles R. Henry, *A General's Insights Into Leadership and Management, Battelle Press,* 1996

Jacobs, Daniel M., *Solicitations, Bids & Proposals*, NCMA, 1990

Jacobs, Daniel M., *The Integrated Project Team (IPT)*, FMP, 2000

Maxwell, John C., *The 21 Indispensable Qualities of a Leader*, Thomas Nelson, Inc., 1999

Packard, David, *The HP Way: How Bill Hewlett and I Built Our Company*, Harper Business, 1995

Pande, Peter S., et.al, *The Six Sigma Way*, McGraw Hill, 2000

PMBOK Guide, Project Management Institute, 4rd Edition, 2009

Powell, Colin, *The Leadership Secrets of Colin Powell*, McGraw-Hill, 2002.

Reports of the President's Blue Ribbon Commission on Defense, GPO, 1986

Slater, Robert, *Jack Welch and the GE Way*, McGraw Hill, 1999

Welch, Jack, et.al, *Winning*, Harper Business, 2005

Womack, James P. and Jones, Daniel T., *Lean Thinking*, Free Press, 2003

INDEX

A
AlliedSignal 26
American Red Cross ix, x, 31, 32
Anderson, Frank iv
Armstrong, Brent iv, 72
Avetissian, Vic iv

B
Babbin, Jed iv
Bannister, Dan ix, x, 13, 30, 51
Beyster, Robert 30, 32, 33, 131
Boeing 102
Bossidy, Lawrence 26
Bowen, Fred iv
BP Capital Management 61

C
Collins, Jim 99, 101, 102, 131
Covey, Stephen R. 7, 117, 131
Computer Sciences Corporation (CSC) 110
Czarny, Mike iv

D
Dallas, Mike iv
Decker, Gerry iv

Defense Contract Management Command (DCMC) 92
Department of Defense (DOD) iii, 13, 28, 92
Dell Computers 12
Dell, Michael 12
Desaulniers, Gene iv
Dole, Elizabeth ix, x, 31, 32
Dota, Paul 32
Drucker, Peter F. 81, 131
Dun & Bradstreet 25
DynCorp iii, v, ix, x, 13, 14, 30, 51

E

F
Fairfield, John iii, iv, v, vi
Fisher, Roger 131
FMG (The Federal Market Group) i, 9, 89, 125, 126
Fogg, C. Davis 41, 131

G
Garlich, Ed iv
Garrett, Greg iv
General Electric ix, x, 6
Gibbs, Joe 23, 24
Gore, Al 92

H

Henry, Charles 92, 131
Hewlett, Bill 23, 24, 132
Hewlett Packard ix, 21, 23, 28, 101

I

J

Jacobs, Daniel i, iv, v, xi, 131, 132
Jacobs, Janet iii

K

Kase, Randy iv
Kloak, Rob 32

L

Lombardi, Vince vii, 129
Lyon, Jack 44, 45

M

Marcus, Idy iv
Marriott, Bill 52
Marriott Corporation 52
McCullough, Eileen 25
McPhee, Don iv
Medley, Ben iv, 110
Milkman, Beverly ix, x, 91, 92

N

National Industries for the Blind (NIB) 92

National Industries for the Severely Handicapped (NISH) 92

O

P

Packard, David ix, 21, 23, 24, 28, 132
Packard Commission Report 28
Performance Results Corporation 72
Perry, Steven iv, ix, x, 72
Pickens, T. Boone 61
Plato 3
PMBOK 103, 104, 105, 108, 109, 110, 112, 132
Powell, Colin 23, 132
President's Committee for Purchasing from the Blind and Severely Disabled ix, x, 91
PriceWaterhouseCoopers 29
Professional Services Council i, 68
Project Management Institute i, 103, 105, 109 132

Q

R

Reagan, Ronald 28
Reid, Tom iv
Reno, William 31, 32
Rider, Jim iv
Ross, Bonnie iv
Rumsfeld, Donald 28

S

Schwab, Charles ix, x, 73
Starke, George iv, 44, 45

T

The Federal Market Group
    (FMG) i, 9, 89, 125,
    126

U

Ury, William 131

V

Vincent, Lenn iv

W

Welch, Jack ix, x, 6, 29,
    39, 132
Wotring, Randy iv
Wrenn, Tom iv

X

Y

Yenrick, Phil iv, 31, 32

Z

CPSIA information can be obtained
at www.ICGtesting.com
Printed in the USA
LVOW13s1304240118
563834LV00019B/375/P